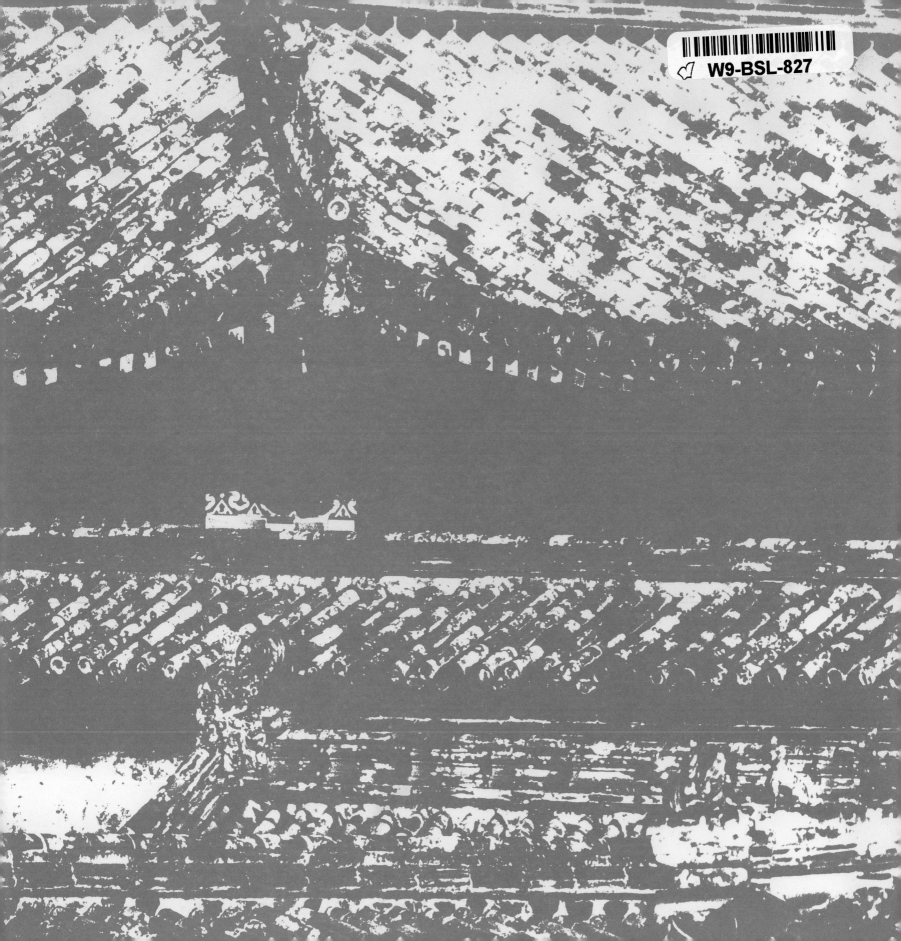

IN THE ORIENTAL STYLE

MICHAEL FREEMAN
SIÂN EVANS
MIMI LIPTON

IN THE

A Bulfinch Press Book

Little, Brown and Company

Boston   Toronto   London

ORIENTAL STYLE

A Sourcebook of Decoration and Design

Page 1   Carved wooden bargeboard from Ban Tab Salak, Thailand.
Title page   Korean medicine chest with Thai hill-tribe basketwork.
Pages 6 and 7   A teashop in Liverpool, in thoroughly traditional
Japanese style; the visual emphasis is upon the use of natural
materials and simple rectilinear forms to promote a
sense of harmony and tranquility.

First North American Edition

ISBN 0–8212–1814–X
Library of Congress Catalog Card Number 90–55397
Library of Congress Cataloging-in-Publication information is
available.

Bulfinch Press is an imprint and trademark of Little, Brown and
Company (Inc.)
Published simultaneously in Canada by Little, Brown and
Company (Canada) Limited

PRINTED IN SINGAPORE

Contents

Since the earliest beginnings of global trade, the West has always looked to the Far East as a fertile source of beautiful objects and exotic materials. Similarly, Occidental architects, artists and designers have used the Orient as a source of inspiration in style and design. This tradition of exchange has reached unprecedented levels in the last ten years, now that Westerners are increasingly able to experience the distant cultures of south-east Asia at first hand, through the growth of cut-price long-haul travel. As the Pacific Basin grows in economic strength and the physical and cultural distance shrinks between East and West, the Orient is now being reappraised as a rich source of both stylistic inspiration and practical solutions in Western interior design.

This book will identify what constitutes 'Oriental' style, both traditional and contemporary, in a variety of indigenous settings, from the relatively well-known ones of China and Japan to the less accessible cultures of Korea, Thailand, Bali and Tibet. It is important to stress that there is no single, definitive 'Oriental' style, but rather a wealth of diverse treatments and approaches. The numerous examples illustrated range from the authentic imitation of traditional interiors to the exuberant, eclectic blending of arts and artefacts from a variety of sources. These diverse themes have been adopted or adapted by Europeans and Americans to create their own, highly personal interpretations of 'Oriental' style.

Throughout this century, it is evident that there have been three approaches to the use and assimilation of the design vocabulary of the Orient. The first consists of the straightforward re-creation of a Far Eastern home and garden, and is mainly confined to the private residences of former expatriates and ardent travellers in the Far East. The second is the natural successor to the enthusiastic response of many nineteenth-century decorators and their clients who used the forms, motifs and colour schemes of the Far East to create an ambience of eye-catching exoticism in a Western setting. As usually neither party had visited the Far East, complete schemes were often created through reference to secondary sources, such as descriptions, photographs, illustrations or imported small-scale objects. The results were occasionally bizarre, but frequently made a strong visual impact. Examples range from the ubiquitous 'sunrise' motif found in domestic and civic architecture throughout Europe and America in the 1920s and 30s (which was 'lifted' from the flag of the Imperial Japanese Navy, via the medium of exported woodblock prints) to the exquisitely lacquered screens of Jean Dunand or the flamboyant, dragon-bedecked exteriors of 'Chinese-style' picture palaces and Asian restaurants.

The third strand is superficially the least overtly 'Oriental' in character. The rational, functional approach of the Modern Movement architects and designers was the logical outcome of a growing sense of recognition of reinterpreted or second-hand traditional Far East solutions in the face of pressing Western problems. In attempting to create simple, inexpensive and flexible domestic environments in the centres of economically depressed and overcrowded cities, where both money and space for new building projects were at a

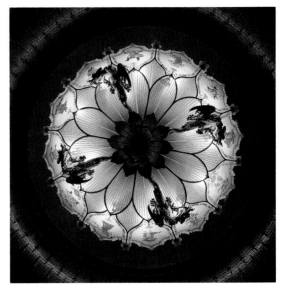

An early nineteenth-century blend of 'Chinese' style crossed with a rococo interpretation of Indian styles, this chinoiserie interior was originally installed in the Brighton Pavilion, but was later removed to Buckingham Palace **(opposite)**. An ornate central light fitting in the Brighton Pavilion features that perennial motif of the Far East, the mythical dragon **(above)**. The inspiration for many 'Orientalist' decorative interiors was taken from designs on imported blue and white Chinese ceramics, such as this cobalt Kangxi jar decorated with insects, flowering plants and stylized rock formations **(below)**.

premium, architects such as Walter Gropius adopted much of the idiom of Far Eastern interior design, such as the use of modules, low-level stacking or folding furniture, built-in storage facilities and curtain walling or screens to create environments which were aesthetically pleasing yet functional and versatile.

The frugal, streamlined simplicity of Modernist urban dwellings is a far cry from the initial impact of the Orient on a delighted but uninformed Western world. As early as the seventeenth century, regular consignments of small, exquisite *objets d'art*, carvings, ceramics, silks and lacquer were reaching Europe, thanks to the efforts and sound business acumen of the traders of Portugal and the Dutch and English East India Companies. Such items excited great curiosity, and were much in demand amongst the nobility and aristocracy of Europe, who prized them for their fine workmanship, luxurious materials and exotic appearance, and chose to display them alongside other social indicators of taste and culture. Although there was a considerable fascination with the countries of their origin, very little was known about the techniques or processes used in their production or, indeed, the nature of the societies producing them. As a result, many disparate artefacts from all over the Far East were indiscriminately labelled 'Chinese', as they had generally been shipped to the West from major ports in southern China.

One of the few Western architects to have first-hand knowledge of China was Sir William Chambers, who had paid a brief visit to Canton and subsequently published his influential book, *Designs of Chinese Buildings, Furniture, Dresses, Machines and Utensils*, in Britain and France in 1757. His famous pagoda at Kew, however, was essentially a Western vision of 'Cathay', rather than a genuine attempt to understand and utilize the forms of China. Fuelled by Chambers' publication, the fashion for chinoiserie grew rapidly among the wealthy; it offered a sense of light-hearted, ephemeral exoticism and intimacy, and therefore was considered to be particularly suitable for small salons, bedrooms and dressing rooms. The decorative motifs typical of this style include mythical beasts, birds and dragons, conventionalized wave and cloud formations and non-representational perspective. Both the iconography and the colour combination of chinoiserie interiors were generally taken from the designs to be found on small-scale Oriental imports, such as lacquer, textiles and porcelain. A small but highly lucrative trade rapidly developed in the direct commissioning of interiors and artefacts from craftsmen in China who were willing and able to produce decorative objects according to designs sent to resident European traders by their wealthy clients in the West. Meanwhile, enterprising European manufacturers catered for the vogue by taking ideas directly from Oriental imports, or by reference to a plethora of trade pattern books to produce 'Chinese' wallpapers, ceramics and furniture to meet public demand.

Chinoiserie provided a constant counterbalance to the rather more austere forms of Neoclassicism then prevalent in Europe and on the eastern seaboard of America; in its delicacy of touch it was more in keeping with the informality and decorative aspects of

European Rococo. Above all, it embodied a romantic exoticism, and as such was particularly favoured as a style for pagodas, summer houses and other 'follies'. The 'Chinese taste' eventually found royal patronage through the Prince Regent's commission for the Brighton Pavilion; due to the exorbitant cost of constructing this building, it became irrevocably linked in the public mind with frivolity and pleasure.

As the nineteenth century progressed, trade between East and West expanded immensely; the colonization of the west coast of America allowed that continent easy access to the bazaars and godowns of Asia, while the opening of the Suez Canal in 1862 halved the dangerous three-month voyage around the Cape which was previously the only shipping route between Europe and the Far East. Western industrialists desperately needed new, lucrative world markets for their mass-produced goods, while Western demand for Oriental art and artefacts remained buoyant.

The continuing appeal of the Orient lay in the undoubted visual allure of many of the objects exported from south-east Asia, combined with a frisson of delight at the sense of the unknown. It cannot be denied that in an era of massive imperial and colonial expansion there was a feeling of pride in the global buying power of the wealthier trading nations, especially among the newly-prosperous middle classes who had profited most from the radical innovations of mass-manufacturing, and the subsequent export of the goods to foreign markets. Paradoxically, it was precisely the same people who still valued the painstaking, labour-intensive crafted artefacts of the Far East; the evident concern with the quality of materials and standards of hand-production to be found in Oriental goods had largely been abandoned as being no longer economically viable in the face of massive industrialization and standardized mechanical production in the factories of Europe and America. The simplicity, refinement and uniqueness of Chinese rosewood furniture, Korean celadon ware or Japanese lacquer struck a chord among those who harboured mixed feelings about the seemingly inevitable march of steam-powered progress.

Until the second half of the century, Oriental imports were generally available only through curio shops or specialist dealers; the artefacts tended to be small in size and exquisite in nature, partly due to their proven saleable value and partly for the more pragmatic reason that each unit took up little space on a long, expensive and arduous sea voyage. Public demand for these goods was also fired by the increasing number of Far Eastern displays at the influential international exhibitions, not least because such settings emphasized the yawning chasm that existed between Far Eastern products and the excessive ornamentation and hybrid styles of their mass-manufactured Western rivals.

In London, the young Arthur Lasenby Liberty bought up a consignment of Japanese goods which had arrived too late to be included in the 1862 Exhibition and founded a retail empire based on the Far Eastern trade; Madame de la Soye of Paris opened 'La Porte Chinoise' and pioneered the wearing of the kimono as a fashionable garment among the

Far Eastern artists realistically portrayed their experience of the burgeoning ports as Oriental trade expanded during the nineteenth century, providing factual records of the growth of major cities; a Chinese export painting of Canton graphically depicts the activity in the American and French concessions **(left above)**, and despite the obvious difference in styles, recalls the almost 'documentary' approach of an earlier Chinese pictorial rug showing the grounds of the Summer Palace **(left below)**. However, romantic visions of the perceived grace, charm and elegance of Oriental life inflamed the creative imaginations of Western artists and designers, because such idyllic images contrasted so strongly with the effects of mass industrialization in their own cultures. A. H. Schramm's *Decorating Buddha's Shrine* **(opposite above left)** and Eliza Turck's *The Doll's Tea Party* **(opposite below)** reveal the fascination which the Orient held for European painters of the nineteenth century. This fascination was extensively transferred into the world of commerce in the Edwardian era, as this commemorative postcard from the Japan-British Exhibition of 1910 testifies **(opposite above right)**.

Spring, Japan-British Exhibition, London, 1910

society ladies of France. Moore of San Francisco imported a variety of decorative artefacts from Asia, which were avidly purchased by Orientophiles. Large department stores followed suit, advertising 'Exotic Goods To Suit All Pockets', and Western manufacturers responded by mass-producing furniture, wallpapers, ceramics and textiles adorned with a bewildering variety of pseudo-Oriental motifs. The Japanese design, in particular, became associated with the theories and practices of the Aesthetic Movement, whose compulsive acquisition of blue and white porcelain (much of it Chinese, in fact) was thoroughly and regularly ridiculed by the satirical magazine *Punch*. By the late 1880s, no self-respecting American or European interior was complete without its complement of Oriental artefacts. Bamboo 'what-nots' of dubious provenance and erratic stability invaded well-to-do drawing rooms, Nanking porcelain jostled for space with hand-painted fans on middle-class mantelpieces, while kimono-clad hostesses poured Chinese tea from Japanese teapots into Spode 'Willow Pattern' cups. The vogue for 'all things Oriental' extended beyond the home; imaginative and frequently lurid novels set in the Far East became best-sellers, Gilbert and Sullivan's *The Mikado* played upon and fuelled the fascination with Japan, and trade journals advertised all manner of pseudo-Oriental wonders, ranging from fake bamboo furniture to 'made-to-measure' water gardens.

The boom in 'Oriental' style at this point was still largely superficial; there was little differentiation in the public mind between the nations of China and Japan, as the names chosen for the characters in *The Mikado* demonstrate. Consequently, the products of many Far Eastern countries were merely grafted on to ornate High Victorian interiors with the aim of creating an atmosphere of exotic eclecticism. However, there were important exceptions to this general rule; a number of influential Western architects and designers were working for wealthy clients whose interest in the Far East was sufficient for them to commission complete 'Orientalist' interiors. Whistler's 'Peacock Room' was a riotous, exuberant combination of Japanese *kimono* motifs with an intense Chinese-style colour scheme of dark blue and gold, the inspiration for this treatment being verbal and written accounts of Buddhist temples.

The eclectic approach to designing interiors from a wide variety of Eastern sources was gradually superseded by the efforts of certain designers to focus upon more appropriate models and to attempt to express the aesthetic values of the cultures which provided their inspiration. E. W. Godwin designed monochromatic interior schemes complete with simple, rectilinear furniture for Japanophile clients such as Oscar Wilde, while the painter Mortimer Menpes travelled extensively through the Far East and commissioned a complete interior of hand-carved Japanese panelling, which was eventually shipped to his London home and installed to house Chinese furniture.

By the beginning of the twentieth century, the random and haphazard use of Far Eastern artefacts as exotic 'props' had fallen from favour with the fashionable, but a wide range of Oriental motifs, colour schemes and technical processes had entered the aesthetic vocabulary

Although the American architect, Frank Lloyd Wright, refused in later years to accept that his innovative 'Prairie House' designs sprang from any Oriental influence, his profound knowledge of Japanese prints, his familiarity with a Japanese pavilion in Chicago and his extensive travels in Japan seem seminal to the development of American architecture, and its subsequent influence on the European 'moderns'. The Pavilion of French Asia at the 1925 Exposition des Arts Décoratifs in Paris **(opposite above)** bears more than a passing resemblance to Wright's 1910 design for a small house for E. C. Waller **(opposite centre)**. Charles Rennie Mackintosh's design for the library of the Glasgow School of Art **(opposite below)** showed a genuine comprehension of Japanese principles of construction allied to a profound understanding of the problems of organizing internal spaces.

of the West. In many cases, a better understanding of Far Eastern approaches, rather than mere mimicry, was evident in the work of innovative designers, artists and architects. The Art Nouveau style was strenuously promoted and publicized in Paris by Siegfried Bing, an avid collector of and dealer in Oriental art, and the sinuous 'whiplash' curves and stylized organic motifs so typical of this movement can be directly traced to a variety of Oriental sources, especially to two-dimensional art and artefacts from Java, China and Japan. However, it was the rectilinear purity and geometrical simplicity of Mackintosh's designs for private residences and the Glasgow Art School that the assimilation, rather than imitation, of Oriental themes, was first evident in Europe.

The Oriental influence on architecture and interior design was stronger in America than in Europe; in particular, the inhabitants of the West Coast had easy access to the Far East, and were more familiar with Asian cultures through the presence of Chinese and Japanese immigrants in the major cities, many of whom sought work as builders or gardeners. The Californian climate facilitated the building of structures similar to those of the Orient, but there was also a strong sense of establishing independence from European culture, a desire to break away from previous traditions in favour of new forms appropriate to life on the Pacific seaboard.

Similarly, Frank Lloyd Wright evolved his influential theories of 'organic architecture' through his intimate knowledge of the graphic art of Japan, his studies of the Japanese Pavilion at the Chicago 1893 World Columbian Exposition, and his travels in Japan. Wright's manipulation of interior space and his concept of 'blurring the boundaries' between the building and its environment were also fundamental characteristics of traditional Far Eastern dwellings. His innovative approach was to be seminal to the future development of domestic architecture throughout the Western world, yet its origins remain unmistakably Oriental.

Westerners living in modern, urban dwellings today are inhabiting this legacy from the Far East; we live in open-plan apartments and we continue to surround ourselves with artefacts traditional or modern from the Orient. We drive Japanese or Korean cars, and wear clothes manufactured in Hong Kong, Singapore or Taiwan. Very few homes are immune to the all-pervasive advance of the Chinese paper lampshade, while Philippino rattan furniture, Thai silks or Indonesian batiks are the mainstay of many modern interiors. For entertainment we listen to miniaturized personal stereos or sit in front of the television to eat a Chinese meal and watch *sumo* wrestling.

The Far East is getting closer and more accessible; it is easier than ever for the average Westerner to reach, and yet familiarity does not, in this case, breed contempt. We are still fascinated by the proliferation of cultures, the decorative forms, vibrant colours and appealing materials of the arts, crafts and artefacts of the countries of south-east Asia and choose to draw upon the region for objects and inspiration in order to create our own 'Oriental Style'.

THE LOOK OF THE ORIENT

The contemporary Far East is a heady and sometimes disconcerting blend of old and new; the essential pragmatism of Oriental peoples has led to the whole-hearted adoption of Western modes of living, but not at the expense of far older, deeper cultural ideals and customs. The ancient, expressed in the stairway of the Japanese shrine **(opposite)**, is revered out of a deep-seated sense of respect for the achievements of one's ancestors, and new ways of living are merely grafted on to time-honoured customs. Although certain governments have recently attempted to preserve the buildings and artefacts of the past, amongst ordinary people there is no feeling that such moves are inappropriate or retrogressive; instead there is a renewed sense of cultural identity and a feeling of pride in their own heritage.

The Look of the Orient is as multifarious as the blanket term 'Oriental' suggests. At first sight there can be few greater contrasts than those which exist between, for example, the thriving, cosmopolitan city of Hong Kong and Lhasa, the remote mountain capital of Tibet. Areas of neon-lit, high-rise Tokyo resemble a set from the film *Blade Runner*, and seem to be a world away from the natural materials, the simplicity and tranquility of rural Thai villages. The ever-increasing size and density of these rapidly-growing cities along Western lines further contributes to the variation in Oriental looks.

However, despite differences in appearance, custom and lifestyle, there is a certain homogeneity of approach among the peoples of eastern Asia – the material, easily quantifiable ways in which people live their day-to-day lives may differ, but there exists a unanimity of fundamental thought which is definitively non-Western, and there are a number of profound similarities between the various countries which manifest themselves in every aspect of daily life.

The first is the massive, all-pervasive influence of China, which can be seen as the historical motherlode of culture throughout the area. The 'Middle Kingdom' evolved standardized systems of weights, measures, coinage and a complex written language of remarkable sophistication; it had laid the foundations of a large, unified Empire under central government several centuries before the birth of Christ. While the Chinese largely regarded themselves as culturally self-sufficient, they were nevertheless avid traders. Vast trade routes reached from the heart of China to the markets of the Roman Empire; finished luxury goods of exquisite workmanship and startling forms and materials travelled along the Silk Routes and fuelled the rumours about the wonders of Cathay which eventually drove Marco Polo in search of the Court of Kubla Khan. Chinese traders also invaded the markets of eastern Asia, dealing in raw materials, spices and finished goods – a constant contact which was to have a profound effect on the neighbouring countries, influencing all fields of life from systems of government, religion, philosophy, written and spoken languages to the indigenous development of literature and the arts. In many respects it is a savage irony that, within living memory, China has attempted to stamp out precisely those values and artefacts which were her major achievements, and had proved to be of such enormous influence beyond her own boundaries.

The Cultural Revolution of 1966–70 was seen by its instigators as a sincere attempt to start again by destroying not only the physical remnants of China's past, but also by completely overturning those values most dominant in the make-up of the Chinese and their Asian neighbours. The Red Guards made strenuous attempts to annihilate deeply ingrained religious and cultural beliefs, such as a profound sense of reverence for the past, the importance of wisdom gained through education and self-improvement, and an unquestioning sense of respect for one's elders and superiors. Although the Chinese authorities have since partially relaxed the policy of completely abnegating the past, at the time of writing

Standing statues of Buddha (above) adorn this traditional Thai temple; Buddhism is a fundamental source of inspiration amongst the peoples of the Far East, and the ideals of non-confrontational co-existence coupled with a desire to improve the lot of oneself and one's family dictates much of the substance of contemporary Oriental life.

Beijing has launched a campaign to rid the capital of 'The Six Evils', one of which is the continuing belief in 'feudal superstition'.

Despite China's recent vigorous efforts to purge herself of the legacy of the past, the second great contributory factor in the 'look of the Orient' is the widespread influence of the great religions throughout Asia, two of which evolved in the Middle Kingdom, and all of which found ready expression in pre-Revolutionary China and permeated south-east Asia through the trading and resulting cultural networks. Taoism and Confucianism are philosophies rather than religions per se; Tao is the Way of the Universe, the struggle to comprehend the supreme motivating force of nature and the order underpinning all life. As such, it teaches veneration for the forces of nature and the necessity of placating those powers through various rituals, magic and alchemy, through which it is believed one can achieve immortality.

The quintessential look of the Orient is achieved by close attention to detail and the constant renewal of traditional craft processes. Examples range from the riotously colourful carved wooden masks of Indonesia **(opposite left)** and the brilliantly hued waxed paper and bamboo parasols of Chiangmai **(opposite right)** to the sympathetic and delicate presentation of food **(above)**. The careful selection of a Japanese fan-shaped dish or Burmese lacquerware to complement the colour and texture of the meal is an indication of the respect paid to the guest and reveals an acute awareness of the desired visual impact. Similarly, meticulous attention to detail is evident in the intricate costume and gestures of the classical Javanese dancer **(below right)**, the restrained opulence of a tiny Fabergé Buddha **(right)**, and the careful wrapping of young trees in a Korean garden **(below)**.

A sense of underlying order, pattern and therefore harmony pervades the look of the Orient; this manifests itself in the symbolic patterns of Japanese raked stone Zen gardens **(left above)** and the understated simplicity of a Thai waterstand **(left below)**.

The concept of an innate order is also common to Confucianism; Confucius believed that at one time, people had lived in a state of social harmony and prosperity – as a result, by following the 'Code for Living', mutual respect and communal progress was attainable. Confucianist ideals are founded upon the value of education, coupled with a sense of respect within the family and, by extension, the broader social unit, leading to an appreciation of human dignity. As a result, age is venerated, whether in people, objects, buildings or institutions. The gradual decay of the outward appearance is more than compensated for by the acquisition of wisdom and experience; hence the need for reliance upon the judgement of one's elders and the adherence to the ways of previous generations, expressed in the practice of ancestor worship.

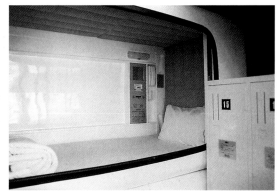

Within Confucianism, strict social hierarchies are observed; women should defer to men, younger brother to elder, son to father. Respect therefore flows up the social pyramid, from female to male, from young to old, employee to employer, individual to authority. The leader of a nation should be the embodiment of Confucian wisdom and virtue, displaying dignity, poise, magnanimity, empathy, a balanced temper and a lack of vulgarity. The population should adhere to the time-honoured rituals and customs of their predecessors and be aware at all times of the appropriate behaviour expected of them. An outburst of bad temper in public or the display of excessive emotion can only lead to the shame of the individual, which is doubly felt by his peers, family or employer. This fear of 'loss of face' exists throughout the region and, as frustrated Western travellers have found, direct confrontation or angry scenes are usually met with implacable stone-walling or frank incomprehension and embarrassment – hence the reputation of Oriental peoples for 'inscrutability' or 'stoicism'. Not only is it considered to be unspeakably vulgar to let down the side, one must also be aware of the problems or restrictions imposed upon the other person; consideration, negotiation, compromise and, above all, tact smooth the path to social success in the Far East as 'face' must be saved by all parties.

Orderly neatness and systematic provision of the necessities of life are evident in the Tokyo 'capsule' hotel **(top)** and the traditional Japanese *o-bento* lunchbox **(above)**.

The third great religion, and perhaps the most influential, is that of Buddhism, which originated in India and subsequently spread throughout Asia. It developed independently in places as far apart as Java and Mongolia and, to the casual observer, there may appear to be little similarity between the Buddhism practised in Japan and that of Burma or Thailand; yet beneath the widely differing external forms there lies a resolute body of doctrine based on the teachings of the Buddha himself.

In brief, the Buddha taught that this life is one of suffering, because of the self-perpetuating nature of physical desires which can never be assuaged. However, through the elimination of desire by meditation, contemplation and the acquisition of wisdom, the mundane can be transcended – the cycle of rebirth provides constant opportunities to reach enlightenment and, eventually, Nirvana. The concept of reincarnation also rules one's attitude to all forms of life, and many devout Buddhists are vegetarian as a matter of course.

Colour and attention to detail abound in all aspects of Oriental life, and are particularly associated with the homes of the wealthy and the decoration of religious structures: Puri Saren Palace, Bali **(opposite)**; the *naga* roof finial of Thailand **(above)**, and the façade of Wat San Pakoi Temple, northern Thailand, at sunset **(right)**.

Buddhists believe that valuable chances to perform meritorious acts are given to them in each life, through not causing unnecessary suffering to any other living thing, through sincerity and honesty, and by sharing what they have with others. The social position and fortunes of any individual are a legacy, and progress through this life is dictated by karma, the results of actions and behaviour in previous existences. Therefore, acceptance of one's lot and genuine attempts to work hard, the need to be responsible and concern with the common good are inherent characteristics of much of Oriental life.

Perhaps given the violence and conflict which have always existed between other world religions, and even within sects of the same religion, the most remarkable aspect of Oriental philosophies and faiths is that they spread so peacefully and influentially, gradually mutating in each culture according to the prevailing social and political climate. Even more surprising is the interchange of new trains of thought with older, indigenous beliefs.

Animism was the oldest and most widespread set of beliefs throughout south-east Asia, and in many of the countries profoundly affected by Taoism, Confucianism or Buddhism, the new beliefs were grafted onto the old ones. Many people today profess to have 'double faiths', although perhaps 'triple' or 'quadruple' might be more accurate. Hong Kong Chinese Roman Catholics pay their respects to their ancestors by burning incense at the temple, and modern Japanese see nothing odd about a couple going through a Shinto wedding ceremony, followed immediately by a Western-style Christian 'white wedding', yet the same family would automatically choose a Buddhist funeral service. Burma is also fundamentally Buddhist, yet most Burmese live in awe of *nats* or spirits. Indeed, Animism continues to exist throughout modern Asia, and is founded upon an understandable respect for the considerable power of nature to damage or destroy all life. Natural phenomena, such as waterfalls, mountains and trees house spirits, provide support and beneficial favours which must be sought by prayers and offerings. Similarly, the dead have immense powers to help or hinder the living, and so their co-operation must be enlisted to ensure a good harvest, an advantageous business deal, a successful marriage.

Physical manifestations of the continuing influence of animism abound throughout the Far East; the colourful and riotous public festivals of Hong Kong, Taiwan and Japan have their roots in the fervent belief of the populace in the need to honour and flatter the god of the harvest, of fertility or of the sea. The importance of shamanistic rituals and the use of fierce-looking demon-faced totem poles outside rural villages in Korea are echoed in the reverence of the Burmese for their *nats*, and the miniature 'spirit houses' found outside every Thai home and business. Japanese traditional buildings frequently feature *onigawara* or demon-faced roof tiles to frighten off bad spirits. Thai temple roof finials are in the form of stylized water serpents, while fierce stone lions protect the entrances of Hong Kong banks.

Mythical beasts abound throughout the Far East, and are believed to embody certain desirable characteristics and provide protection against evil forces; the guardian lion is a motif found throughout the Forbidden City of Beijing **(opposite above)**, while the dragon epitomizes strength and integrity and is thus portrayed on the eaves of the Pulguk-sa Temple in South Korea **(opposite below)**. The fascinating intricacy of the roof **(right)** of the Maha Muni Temple Pagoda in Mandalay, Burma, reveals the astonishing commitment to skilled craftsmanship which can be found on temple buildings throughout the region.

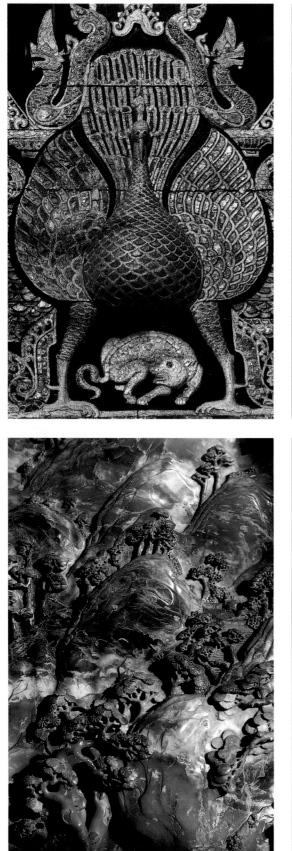

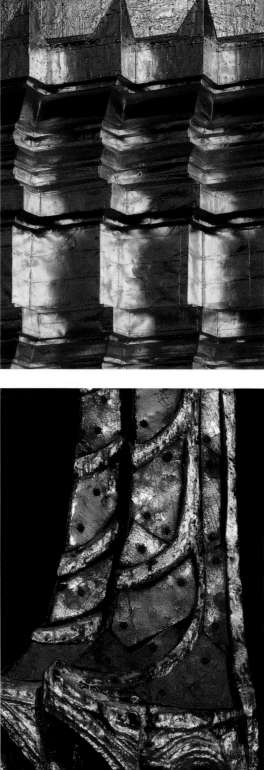

The ornately decorative use of precious metals in glowing colours is widespread in much of Oriental architecture. In contrast to Western values, the lavish ornamentation of the exterior of a building in the East commands respect for the institution and the individuals responsible for it, rather than envy or derision at such ostentation. In Thailand, especially, the practice of donating money to enable the further decoration and refurbishment of the local Buddhist temple is still considered a meritorious act. Consequently, the state of a temple is often a more accurate indicator of local prosperity than the seemingly humble dwellings grouped around it.

The combination of gold or gilt with brilliantly-coloured enamels or inlaid stones is particularly prevalent in Burma and Thailand; certain examples, such as the Wat Rajabopit in Bangkok **(opposite)**, also reveal a profound influence from India. The gilded, relief-moulded peacock of Wat Pan Thao **(above left)** guards the doorway to the *viharn* or assembly hall, and a carved wooden window frame in the same complex is ornamented with gold inlaid with mica fragments **(below right)**. A detail from the golden *chedi* of Wat Haripunchai in northern Thailand **(above right)** forms a fascinating sequence of undulating columns, while a jade boulder **(below left)** from the Jewellery Hall of the Forbidden City reveals an exquisitely worked, stylized, classical Chinese landscape.

As the magical properties of certain beasts and birds are believed to be able to withstand possible assaults from the forces of evil, animal imagery and symbolism is an essential aspect of the look of the Orient. Imaginary mythological and zoomorphic forms adorn every surface of religious significance, such as the *garuda* (half-bird, half-man) of Bali or the *erewan*, the three-headed elephant god of Thailand. However, less fantastic animals are also credited with protective or aspirational characteristics. The stork traditionally symbolizes purity, the bat stands for happiness and ducks are the epitome of monogamy, fidelity and hence, happy marriages. Similarly, the twelve animals of the Chinese horoscope are believed to impart certain characteristics to people born within their span, and also to govern the lives of all during their cycle of ascendancy.

The most evocative symbol of the Far East, and the one which has been used most avidly by Western artists and designers in their reinterpretations of Oriental style, is the dragon. In ancient China, the property and person of the Emperor were symbolized by the five-toed dragon, and it remains a potent image to many people in the Far East. Chinese mythology holds that mountains contain sleeping dragons and that in order to choose successfully the best site for a building, one should be anxious to avoid antagonizing the slumbering reptile. Instead, it is possible to use his strength and vitality by building in accordance with the layout of the site, harnessing the dragon's breath or *chi* by referring to the ancient art or science of

The intricacy of pattern and detailing to be found in Oriental crafts is especially appealing to Western eyes; the textures and forms of this selection of woven Thai baskets **(left)** are based upon traditional practices, yet the designs are fresh and immediate. Such baskets make wonderfully decorative additions to any interior.

geomancy. The concept of beneficial placement still has a profound hold over Chinese inhabitants of Hong Kong, Taiwan and the Philippines and, indeed, is gaining some credence in the West. Briefly, *feng shui* literally means 'wind and water', and consists of the identification of certain physical factors in a given site for the success of a business venture or the building of a home.

The original design of Norman Foster's Hong Kong and Shanghai Bank was substantially modified on the advice of *feng shui* experts, because it was felt that the energy inherent to the locale would drain from the building. Even on a domestic scale, the proportions of furniture, the ideal height of shelving and the location of mirrors is dictated by the principles of *feng shui*. For example, it is rare in a traditional-style Chinese house to have the main staircase leading directly to the front door, as fortune and prosperity are believed to flow out. Instead, the door will be situated at an angle to stop the loss of good luck, and a large piece of furniture, such as a table, will be placed in the hallway to provide a foil against the egress of positive energy.

To further ensure the superiority of beneficial aspects over less agreeable ones, many Oriental peoples refer to the state of ideal balance and harmony known as *yin* and *yang*, the complementary forces which underpin all things. *Yin* elements are considered to be feminine, and are characterized by darkness, cool colours, liquidity, space or void, and even numbers.

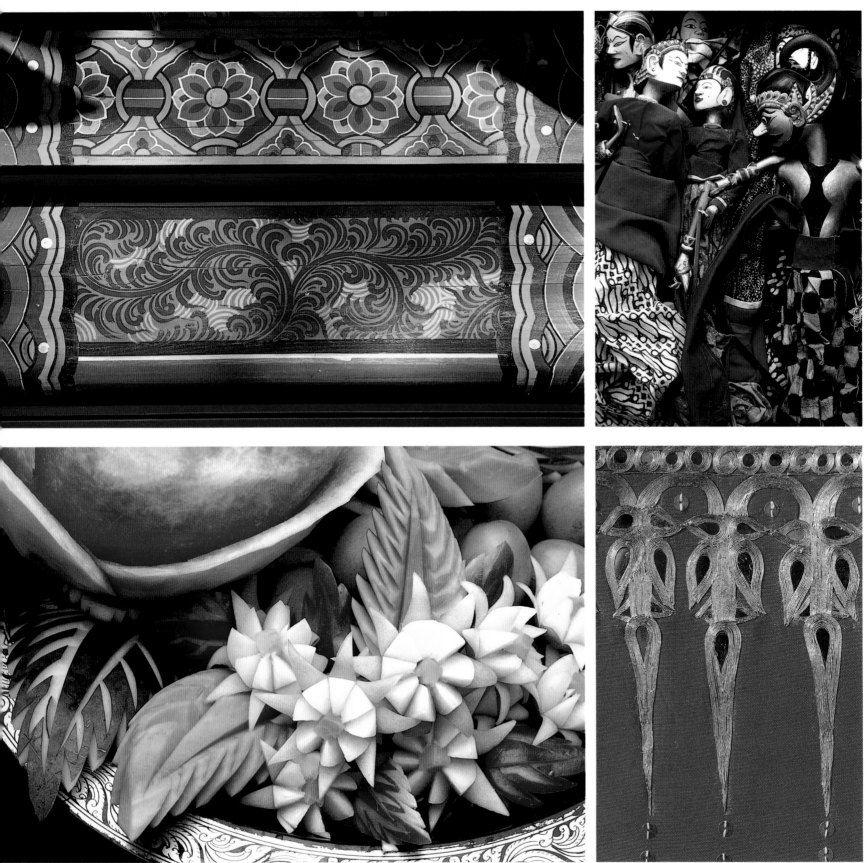

Colourful naturalistic motifs abound in Oriental arts and crafts, reflecting the interdependence of man and the environment. Brilliantly-hued patterns of stylized plants and flowers adorn windows in a South Korean temple **(right above)**, and also feature in Indonesian glass **(right below)**. Colour and pattern derived from the natural world recur in a multiplicity of artefacts from the Orient: a painted panel from Korea **(opposite above left)**; the exquisite fruit and vegetable carving of Thailand **(opposite below left)**; puppets from Indonesia **(opposite above right)**; silk from Chiangmai **(opposite below right)**.

Yang forces are regarded as masculine, typified by brightness, warm colours, solidity, depth and odd numbers. The ideal environment is therefore a blend of *yin* and *yang*, which promotes concord, harmony and progress, as well as being easy on the eye. To take the example of a modern building; the structure is *yang*, because it is a semi-solid form, but it should be surrounded by space in the form of a courtyard, whose harsher boundaries are softened by vegetation and, ideally, flowing water, to counterbalance the dominance of the structure. Although Chinese in origin, the dual ideas of *feng shui* and *yin* and *yang* are also found in the location of ideal burial sites in Korea, and in the creation of traditional Japanese stone gardens. Ryoanji in Kyoto consists of a raked gravel area representing the ever-changing nature of water, while large boulders represent islands, symbolizing continuity and integrity.

Idealized landscapes, combining water and mountains, permeate much of the artistic life of the Far East, ranging from the laborious cultivation of bonsai to the stylized representation of soaring mist-clad mountains and waterfalls in traditional Chinese art. The symbolic strength of water is a recurrent theme in the look of the Orient – like all natural phenomena, water was believed to be invested with the power for good over evil, yet could decimate and destroy with little apparent concern for human life. So much of traditional Oriental living was dependent upon the cycles of the harvests, especially rice, which needs plenty of fresh rain water at a crucial stage in its development. The fine balance between flooding and drought was a matter of constant concern to the inhabitants of the Yangtse flood-plain. To Thais living in Bangkok, water provides not only a means of transport but a livelihood, while Hong Kong junk-dwellers regard it as home and modern Japanese live in fear of a *tsunami* or major tidal wave. Water is therefore frequently featured in the decorative arts, and is also regarded as a vital, purifying force. Khmer temples are reached by ascending a series of man-made terraces, each with its own 'cleansing' pond, and the celebrations of the Burmese New Year in April are marked by the apparently random throwing of buckets of water over all surfaces and unfortunate passers-by.

New Year is the most auspicious date in the Oriental calendar, and as such is the occasion on which traditional practices and rituals are most avidly followed. In preparation for the great day, houses and business premises must be thoroughly cleaned, and all outstanding debts must be paid – indeed, wealthier people often distribute small sums of cash to ensure that they have not inadvertently failed to repay a debt. Damaged household goods like chipped ceramics or shabby furnishings must be thrown away to be certain of good fortune and prosperity in the coming year. The occasion itself is marked in different ways throughout the region – seething dragons dance through the streets of Hong Kong and Taiwan, or indeed, through predominantly Chinese districts around the world, while far-flung Japanese will make strenuous attempts to return to the home of the head of their family in order to pay their respects and go to the temple together.

Two-dimensional patterned surfaces from the countries of the Far East frequently take naturalistic forms as their inspiration; often, the subject matter portrayed is highly abstract and therefore to Westerners it no longer carries a symbolic value. Pictured here **(opposite)** are a variety of textile designs from Indonesia and Thailand, with a ceramic wall panel of dragons from Beijing.

The plethora of traditional forms, motifs and finishes displayed in the window of a ceramics shop in Seoul **(left)** betrays a variety of indigenous and foreign styles, but paramount throughout the region is the all-pervasive influence of pre-revolutionary China, which can be seen as the cultural motherlode of the Far East, a power expressed in the Meridian Gate **(opposite)** of the Forbidden City, Beijing (detail).

The look of the Orient is dictated by this strange blend of cultural and religious heritage alongside the preoccupations of everyday life; unlike the peoples of the West, most Orientals see their religion, philosophy and faith as an intrinsic part of ordinary life. Mendicant Buddhist monks are frequently seen on the streets of cities and villages and are unquestioningly supported by the local inhabitants. Valuable business deals are amicably arranged in restaurants over lavish, beautifully presented meals without overt reference to the matter at hand, as both parties tacitly agree the terms and conditions by being aware of the needs of the other and realizing the necessity of fulfilling their own obligations. The *Tong Shu*, or Chinese Almanac, is avidly consulted by many for a day-to-day horoscope, and personal forecasts and palm-readings are conducted in temple grounds. The advice of a *feng shui* geomancer may be claimed against tax, and a flurry of financial activity can be expected on any date which has the fortuitous figure eight in it; in Hong Kong, the 8th of August 1988 saw an unprecedented number of new companies being officially registered, contracts were ceremoniously signed after months of deliberation and large numbers of young couples were married.

Traditional Oriental culture is tenacious; it thrives amidst the world's most populous and rapidly-changing cities, even though the rural way of life is gradually disappearing, and despite the fact that the vast conurbations of the Far East seem initially to have more in common with their Western equivalents. Under the veneer of internationalism, the look of the Orient is the physical manifestation of the profound strength of cultural heritage. The appearance of the man-made environment is a reflection of fundamental attitudes to the natural order, and the way in which people live is based upon centuries-old beliefs in the religions and philosophies of the area. Evil spirits must be guarded against, unlucky numbers are to be avoided, and respect must be paid to one's elders and betters; it is important not to rock the communal boat, and yet every member of society has a duty to improve the fortunes of the family through hard work and the acquisition of experience and wisdom. Some Westerners bemoan the apparent rapid passing of the old ways, but the truth is that much of Oriental life is based upon a sense of pragmatism coupled with a genuine belief that past, present and future are a continuous stream – to fight against this current is futile, but instead one must keep moving with it to ensure the best for the future.

A continuing belief in animism, or the power of spirits over the living, is evident in the Shinto ceremonies of Japan **(opposite)**, the positioning of terrifying totem poles outside rural Korean villages to frighten off demons **(above right)**, and the effigy heads of Toradjan **(below right)**.

The *naga* or mythical water serpent of Thailand is the favoured form of roof finials for temples **(left)**, so that the structure may be protected against evil spirits bent on destroying the building; however, the aid of benevolent forces is also enlisted, as in the offerings to promote fertility made at a Buddhist temple in Kamakura, Japan **(below)**.

The showroom of a lacquer works in Ho Chi Minh City shows the multiplicity of forms and finishes available in the medium. The process of lacquering **(opposite far left)** is lengthy and heavily labour-intensive, so individual craftsmen frequently specialize in one stage only of the production before passing the piece on to another member of the team.

Wooden components are first shaped and smoothed to form a suitable base, and are then hand painted with the sap of the *rhus vernicifera* tree. Each piece must be laid flat and protected from dust and light as it is allowed to dry between applications; it is then polished, dusted and recoated. The best quality lacquer is the result of as many as thirty individual coats, and this constant process of burnishing and layering gives lacquerware its characteristic glowing subtlety.

There are a variety of finishes available in lacquerware; incised or carved decoration is common, especially in China where the recessed areas are painted in subtle pastel shades. Japanese lacquer objects are often decorated with sprinkled metallic dust or small squares of gold and silver in an apparently random pattern. Another popular decorative technique involves the application of delicately carved slivers of mother-of-pearl to create a pattern of stylized, symbolic plant and animal forms.

The ancient craft of batik is a method of dyeing woven cotton by exploiting the impermeable properties of wax to the vegetable dyes traditionally used throughout the Far East. Intricate patterns are traced on to a length of fabric, and these outlines or blocked areas are redefined in wax. The length is then dyed, and the pattern is created as a negative image, because the waxed areas retain their original colour. Wax will then be applied in a slightly different pattern, and this process is repeated many times until the definition of the decorative design through the over-dyeing of different colours has reached the desired level of sophistication. The characteristic 'crackle' texture of batik fabric is caused by the occasional splitting of the waxen surface during handling and redyeing; this allows small quantities of colour to penetrate the fabric along the fracture line.

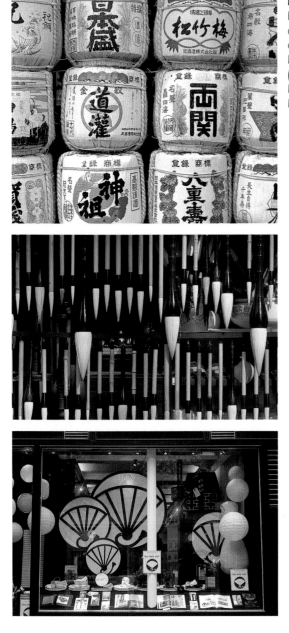

Display and presentation of even the most humble market vegetables is an integral factor in determining the look of the Orient; sake barrels, calligraphy brushes and ceramics are stacked deep but with a view to displaying them at their best **(left and below)**, a format successfully adopted by both a London retail store **(bottom left)** and a Bangkok antiques emporium **(right)**.

The use of repetitive structural components to create a sense of visual unity is a particular feature of Oriental architecture, both traditional and modern. The use of a three-dimensional pattern found on the façade of an ancient Thai temple **(opposite left)** is reiterated in the modular construction of a Tokyo capsule hotel **(opposite right)** and the temple roof of a palace in Seoul **(right)**.

TRADITIONAL LIVING

The construction methods and resulting forms of traditional Far Eastern domestic building are, naturally, a response to the local and climatic requirements; the choice of materials is more a matter of easy availability and proven durability than of idealism. Far Eastern homes vary considerably in style and structure, but they also express the deeper preoccupations and aspirations of each culture. As such, the traditional Oriental house is the physical manifestation of fundamental philosophies, religions and cultural beliefs.

Where the climate allows it, the traditional Oriental dwelling is opened to its surroundings as much as possible, creating a sense of harmony with the environment, shown here in a nineteenth-century Chinese painting **(above)**.

The vernacular house in any culture is the result of a number of factors dictated by two major criteria; firstly, it is intended to provide shelter from the elements, and secondly its form is created by the relative ease of access to suitable local building materials. However, it is also a reflection of the beliefs and aspirations of its inhabitants, so its final form can be said to embody the nature of the society which produced it.

A wide diversity of traditional housing types exists in the Far East, and at first sight a stone-built Tibetan dwelling appears to have very little in common with the wooden stilt housing of Thailand. However, there is a fundamental homogeneity of approach to domestic building throughout the countries of south-east Asia. As in other countries, Far Eastern housing is the culmination of a strong, historical-cultural tradition, refined over many years of social evolution. The form and structure of the traditional Oriental house is often centuries-old, but the design is subtly modified and developed every time it is passed on to the next generation in those societies which have a strong sense of the past and retain an implicit respect for the old ways as an essential element in their attitude to life.

Needless to say, much of the traditional housing of the Far East is fast disappearing; as the area rapidly adopts industrialization along Western lines, the drift to the cities becomes more pronounced. And not only is the desire for simple vernacular housing declining but the skilled craftsmanship needed to produce it is also being dissipated. Wealthy urban Asians now aspire to the materials, styles and gadgetry of the West and, until recently, it seemed as though the traditions of the past would be lost forever. However, within the last decade a number of Oriental governments have taken steps to deliberately retain and promote their cultural heritage by preserving buildings of particular interest or beauty. Initially, this momentum was provided by the increase in tourism to the Far East, but increasingly it reflects a genuine attempt to protect and foster an important sense of national identity and pride, perhaps symptomatic of the growing economic strength and prosperity of the Far East.

The unifying factor underlying the form of traditional Oriental building is the profound and widespread influence of religion, particularly Buddhism. According to Buddhist teachings, this life is merely a transitory phase in our total existence, and consequently the home should be regarded as a temporary shelter which provides a sanctuary for the body while the soul attempts to achieve enlightenment. The Buddha found enlightenment while resting under a tree; consequently, the form of much Oriental building consists of a lightweight wooden pillar-and-beam construction rising from a solid, well-defined base, and overhung by extended eaves providing shade and shelter for the family.

The emotional or psychological role played by the traditional roof is emphasized by the various decorations applied to the structure. In Thailand, the simplest dwelling has a roof surmounted with *naga* or carved finials in the form of stylized flames or animal forms, while in Korea and Japan the gable end is often terminated by grotesque ceramic tiles featuring devils' faces to ward off evil spirits. Regardless of the prevailing religion, there still exists a

Overhanging eaves protect the structure and create a verandah area which not only blends the transition between artificial structure and natural setting, but also provides an important forum for family life. Exterior walls are frequently no more than removable screens; hence, the lives of the inhabitants are enriched by the opportunities to contemplate the changing seasons, and reinforcing the sense of respect for the considerable power of natural forces in countries prone to the vagaries of tempestuous weather. These three examples are from different countries: Korea **(right)**, Thailand **(right below)** and Vietnam **(below)**.

The spreading eaves, soaring gables and low-pitched roofs of rural South Korean homes betray a major stylistic influence from China. Yet in their pillar-and-beam construction, their overhanging roofs and curtain-walling, they are also physical manifestations of the Buddhist belief that this existence is merely transitory, and that the home should therefore be considered as a temporary shelter, a physical base from which to seek spiritual enlightenment. The Buddha gained enlightenment while resting under a tree, and the 'parasol' structure of much traditional domestic building throughout the region can be likened to the shelter provided by groves of trees, which can provide a refuge from the stresses, strains and storms of everyday life. The metaphor is heightened by the overt use of unadorned timber and barely-finished tree trunks to make up the visible skeleton of the building.

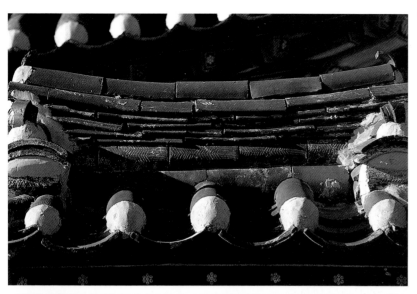

Traditional Oriental roofs are solidly built and exude an air of protective security, as do these examples from Korea; the wellbeing of the structure and inhabitants is ensured by the use of roof finials, three-dimensional sculptures or ceramic tiles in the form of devils' faces, to ward off evil spirits **(left)**. By contrast, the walls of the structure conform to a standard of rectilinear simplicity **(below)**.

fundamental belief in good and bad forces, which can be averted or placated by the appeal of the inhabitants to the stronger protective powers of other spirits, frequently epitomized as animals; for example, the fish is considered in many cultures to be a natural protector from fire, which is understandably feared by the inhabitants of wooden buildings; consequently, fish motifs frequently occur in architectural carvings.

The prevalence of animal or anthropomorphic decorative forms in traditional building is also indicative of the sense of dependence on the natural environment felt by many peoples of south-east Asia, and this concept dictates the form of structures in those countries where the climate allows the inhabitants to live in closer harmony with their environment. In Thailand, southern Korea and Japan, the house is open to the elements as exterior walls are frequently little more than removable screens; this practice blurs the boundaries between the house and its surroundings, creating a sense of the structure 'belonging' to the landscape, rather than squatting upon it. Local, natural materials such as wood, clay, thatch and plaster are therefore preferred for the structure, and often these elements appear to be rough-hewn or even 'unfinished' to Western eyes. Supporting beams are deliberately left to look like tree trunks, and large boulders frequently form the path or steps up to the house, reinforcing the sense of at-oneness between habitation and environment.

This deep-rooted empathy with Nature is also a result of the widespread, healthy respect for the considerable power of natural forces throughout south-east Asia. The climate in countries such as China, Korea and Japan can vary greatly throughout the year, and so the traditional houses of these regions have evolved as extremely adaptable, functional dwellings. Low-pitched structures with extended overhanging eaves are designed to withstand the weight of considerable snowfalls, while a heavily-thatched or tiled roof provides good insulation against both sub-zero temperatures and intense summer heat. Humidity can also be a major problem in Thailand, the Philippines and Japan, so a house surrounded by a shaded verandah and loosely bounded by mobile 'curtain' walls enables the inhabitants to open the interior, allowing breezes through the structure, while work, leisure and entertainment is conducted on the raised verandah, shaded from the worst of the sun.

The lightweight construction and ease of access to the exterior is also a real necessity in Oriental countries where earthquakes and consequent fires are a constant threat. The traditional Japanese house is built of wooden pillars and beams; the structural elements extend and overlap each other like intertwined fingers, and the joints are held together by wedge-shaped pegs of wood. The result is a flexible skeleton; under the considerable torsion caused by an earthquake, the frame will yield to conflicting strains but will stay intact. After the tremors have subsided, the pegs can be hammered back into position and the building will revert to true. Similarly, the construction of a building as a series of interconnected outbuildings or pavilions, linked by covered walkways and roofed but open corridors, allows component parts of the building to flex independently during an earthquake without

In the hotter, more humid countries, traditional buildings enable the inhabitants to withstand the climate by providing what is effectively a series of interconnected roofs supported by pillars and subdivided by curtain walls. The various components of the home are linked by covered walkways, as in the Kamtheing House, Bangkok **(opposite)**. Trees and vegetation grow between the split-level terraces, and the blurring of boundaries between the house and the landscape is also apparent in the variety of undecorated natural woods used as building materials. A simple teak door-latch **(below right)** has an intrinsic sculptural appeal, while the weathered exterior of a temple meeting-house **(above left and above right, below left)** is a testament both to the pride of local carpenters and the vicissitudes of the climate.

The free flow of air between exterior and interior is essential for traditional homes in hotter climates; consequently, open-plan wooden corridors and pillared façades and balustrades on external walls are typically found in Thai buildings **(above left and above right)**.

jeopardizing the whole structure, an approach adopted successfully by the American architect Frank Lloyd Wright in his radical design for the Imperial Hotel, Tokyo.

In countries where earthquakes are relatively uncommon but the major problem is that of surviving freezing winter temperatures and heavy snowfalls, such as in Tibet or the northernmost parts of China, traditional houses are compact and solid-walled with well-insulated roofs. Nevertheless, they also tend to follow the general pattern of a complex of buildings grouped around a central courtyard; the outer facades have few windows or doors to minimize the loss of heat to the exterior, and the main access for traffic and light is located within the central well. The traditional Chinese *pingfang*, or one-storeyed house, is typically built as a three-sided, U-shaped structure around a central courtyard; protection is thus ensured both from the vagaries of the extreme climate and the curious gaze of casual passers-by.

Throughout the Far East, the main entrance to a home is usually less prominent than Westerners might expect; indeed, it is often difficult positively to identify the size or extent of the home from the outer boundaries of the site, as natural and cultivated vegetation is usually encouraged to grow up to and between the complex of 'pavilions' which make up the house. Buildings are often constructed around the natural features of the site, such as large rocks or mature trees. The orientation and location of the home is influenced by a number of

factors; in those countries with a strong Chinese-influenced cultural history, the ancient art or science of *feng shui* still has a firm hold on the national consciousness, and at the planning stage the advice of the local *feng shui* man is considered essential in order to maximize the positive qualities of a site. Geomancy stresses the necessity of capitalizing upon prevailing natural forces to ensure the success, prosperity and happiness of the inhabitants. Animism or shamanism, the belief that spirits reside in natural forms and can profoundly affect the physical, financial and mental health of humans, is still prevalent in rural areas of Korea and Japan, and these views do not clash with the rather more orthodox religions existing in those countries.

Rather more practical considerations tend to dictate the siting of those few rooms with a specific and unique function; the kitchen will ideally be located at the furthest point from the toilet, which is situated downwind of the main body of the house for reasons of hygiene; nevertheless, the toilet is known colloquially as the 'Devils' Corner' in some Far Eastern cultures when the wind changes direction. The other rooms tend to have a less specific function; the main entrance is defined by a broad step which enables the visitor to get on to the verandah, having first discarded his footwear in order not to bring dirt into the interior. There is generally a reception room immediately adjacent to the entrance, where a guest is provided with food, drink and a welcome rest. While the majority of Far Eastern housing is

Interior room divisions are also designed to allow the circulation of breezes; in the case of this old house in Bangkok, one segment of a panelled wall can be slid aside, affording a view of the next room **(above left and above right)**.

The layout of Thai buildings generally consists of a sequence of structures, linked by verandahs and covered walkways. The verandahs of this ancient house in Bangkok allow access between the rooms without infringing on the inhabitants' privacy **(left above and left below)**. Carved wooden panelling **(opposite)** and slatted windows create an air of ordered simplicity, and are a testament to the skills of the craftsmen who constructed the house.

unostentatious and simple, the 'guest room' is often decorated with a small number of simple and carefully-chosen objects arranged as focal points to stimulate contemplation and a sense of aesthetic pleasure; these items are designed to be viewed while sitting on the floor, and consequently their display is different from what might be expected in the West.

One overriding characteristic of traditional Oriental housing is the flexibility and sense of space to be found in the interior. The rooms are usually decorated in unadorned natural materials and are largely unfurnished, allowing the inhabitants extensively to use the space available for a wide variety of their everyday activities. The simplicity and even austerity of taste derived from the Buddhist philosophy means that much of the family's life is conducted while seated on mats or cushions, on the floor of the rooms or on the verandah, as the climate dictates. Furniture is therefore constructed to a height suitable for use while seated on the floor, but is generally kept to a minimum and can often be stacked or stored when not in use. The larger, less mobile pieces are those used for storage. Rural Chinese dwellings often contain little more than a number of large wooden beds and a couple of chests or dressers, which house family belongings. Even beds and bedding are often portable, and the inhabitants sleep by night in rooms which are utilized fully for other purposes by day. Consequently, sleeping areas are frequently defined by only the most elementary of partitions or portable screens.

Folding or free-standing screens can be found in one form or another throughout the Orient; they are extremely versatile and adaptable pieces of furniture, and often beautiful in their own right. In colder climates, they provide welcome windbreaks against draughts and enhance the effect of various traditional forms of heating such as the Japanese *hibachi* or brazier, the built-in stove of China or the Korean system of underfloor heating, known as *ondol*. When not required for these purposes, they provide some privacy for the inhabitants, and can also be used as decorative backgrounds for festive occasions.

The interior of many traditional homes is notionally subdivided by sliding doors or walls; in hotter climates, latticework or carved wooden transom panels immediately below ceiling level allow the circulation of air; they are often highly decorative, featuring intricate geometric patterns or stylized plant and animal forms. To add to the light and airy effect of Korean and Japanese interiors, translucent hand-made rag or rice paper is pasted across latticework windows and interior partitions; this allows a subtle diffusion of light, but provides little noise reduction between one room and another.

To many Westerners, the idea of an individual's privacy within the home is jealously guarded; in our culture, small children who share a bedroom with their siblings frequently cherish an ambition of having their 'own room' and, their ambition realized, will define their territory with their own belongings. The layout of the traditional Far Eastern house militates against the 'selfish' concerns of the individual in favour of the common good and cohesion of the family group. The central precept of Confucianism is that filial piety is the basis of all

The interior of a traditional-style Balinese house epitomizes the Oriental principle of revealing the structure through the deliberate exposure of building components, thereby enhancing the sensation of flowing space. The skeleton of the house becomes a fascinating sculpture; a minimalist staircase leads into the living room, and rugged ceiling beams interlock **(opposite above and opposite below)**.

The living rooms open onto the garden and are furnished with low-level pieces produced by local craftsmen in a variety of native materials. The resulting atmosphere is almost reminiscent of summerhouses and garden pavilions **(above and left)**.

In traditional Oriental rural dwellings, the kitchen is one of the few rooms with a specific, clearly-defined function; furthermore, it often provides the focal point for the informal activities of the household.

As in the rest of the house, there is little in the way of furniture or fittings in the Western sense; most food preparation and cooking is done while squatting on mats on the floor, and so the cooking ranges are at a suitably low level. In Korean farmers' kitchens **(opposite above and below left)** small serving tables which act as individual trays for meals are stacked on one side when not needed, while handwoven baskets of assorted sizes are piled up on a shelf at eyelevel; decorative *sake* containers are stored on a chest **(opposite below right)**. Similarly, in a traditional Thai kitchen **(right)**, unnecessary utensils are slung overhead in a suspended rack, although those implements in constant use remain within easy reach. Dry goods, cooking oils and perishable foodstuffs must be kept safe from marauding insects and animals, so they are stored in large ceramic jars with tight-fitting lids.

Adequate ventilation in the kitchen is essential, especially in those parts of the Far East where the weather becomes very hot and humid during the summer. It is therefore common in houses of this kind to find the windows unglazed and unscreened; the Thai kitchen is located at the corner of the structure so that two windows set at right angles to each other maximize the effects of any passing breezes.

The drawing room wing of a mansion in South Korea is almost devoid of fixed pieces of furniture so that the space may be used in a versatile way; dividing panels are suspended from the ceiling until required.

conduct, and there is a clearly-defined social hierarchy in the Far East determined by age and gender. Consequently, every member of the family is aware of their position, and so potential conflicts tend to be avoided. Confucianism also teaches reverence for the wisdom and experience of one's elders, and this colours attitudes towards all forms of authority and interpersonal relationships. In many parts of rural south-east Asia the home is also the workplace, and the family occupation tends to benefit from the sense of co-operation engendered by constantly living in such proximity, particularly in those cultures where the apprenticeship system ensures the handing-down of vital skills.

This sense of corporate effort for the common good is found on a wider scale in the construction of traditional housing, as the extended family and neighbours frequently combine forces to erect a new home or to repair an existing one. The group provide the manual labour under the leadership of a local skilled builder; it is only recently and still comparatively rarely that a professional architect or designer in the Western sense of the term has been employed to decide the finished form of the building according to the client's brief. Instead, the choice of a site and orientation of the structure may be advised by a *feng shui* geomancer, and the family will decide what and where to build according to the group's requirements and means.

The proportions of the structure may be determined by the availability of pre-fabricated components according to a traditional modular system; in Burma, the module is 6 feet by 2 feet, the unit considered sufficient space for an adult to sleep on in comfort. In Japan the equivalent module is 6 feet by 3 feet, the size of a *tatami* mat, and the size of a room may be described by the number of mats in it. The considerable benefits of both building to a pre-determined module and of constructing a house as a series of linked rooms is the ease with which the structure can be extended if the family's size and fortunes expand proportionately in later years, and repairs can more easily and quickly carried out if the house is damaged by the vicissitudes of nature. Wherever possible, the new structure will be almost identical to the old out of a sense of reverence for the past and a genuine desire for almost seamless continuity. Visitors to Japan are particularly struck by the fresh appearance of buildings which are ostensibly hundreds of years old – in fact, they are frequently the latest in a series of exact replicas; the materials may be only fifty years old, but to the Japanese the total structure is a thoroughly archaic, historical building.

The sense of group co-operation for the good of the community is engendered by the need to work together to bring in the harvest, the success of which determines the survival of the community for another year. The ownership of land is dear to the heart of rural Oriental

The simple, low-level furnishings, the lack of ostentation and the reliance upon natural materials in a traditional administrative office in Korea create an effect of harmonious tranquility, suitable for an unobtrusive working environment.

Sleeping arrangements vary throughout the region depending upon the climate and local customs; in this traditional rural house outside Bangkok **(left)**, the 'bedroom' as Westerners understand the term does not exist. The sleeping area is designated by the provision of simple flat mattresses which fold up when not required, and curtains give some privacy. Ventilation comes through the unglazed window, which also has wooden shutters, and a large mosquito net protects the inhabitants from that local scourge.

This house in Chiangmai contains a low Thai bedstead in teak. The carved wooden pediment forming the bedhead is an example of architectural salvage, and the design is typical of the 'flame' configuration found on much of the traditional architecture of Thailand. The outline of the carving suits the high-pitched ceiling of the room.

The sequence of buildings which make up the Rinshun-kaku of Yokohama are the epitome of traditional Japanese architecture. Originally constructed in 1649, they are wooden structures with heavy overhanging eaves. The interior space **(above)** is subdivided by sliding *fusuma* (screens), frequently decorated with exquisite paintings such as *Wild Geese* by Eitoku Kano. The *fusuma* can be removed from their grooves to create a large interior space, softly lit by the translucent *shoji*.

peoples, and it is interesting to note that in a number of cases it was the prospect of overturning the existing feudal control of the land that provoked major social change, as in the Chinese Revolution, and in Occupied Japan immediately after World War II. However, rural farmers do not believe that they 'own' their land in the same way that their Western counterparts do; instead they believe that they are 'looking after it' for their family. Consequently, it is considered in some cultures to be a major disgrace to sell or lose the ancestral home, and heads of families have been known to commit suicide if faced with the sale of the family house to meet debts.

The family's ancestors are believed to be perpetually present within the building, keeping a watchful eye on the present generation and guiding and advising them when necessary, so daily offerings are made to their memory. The local spirits thought to reside in the area are both feared and respected by inhabitants of traditional Oriental homes, so they are courted and placated by the family. The boundaries of Korean villages are frequently marked along the roadsides by massive, carved wooden totem poles with frightening faces to ward off evil

forces, while 'spirit houses', miniature models of the building, can be found outside Thai dwellings to house beneficent entities. Thais plant groves of trees for them to live in, and Japanese farmers will often bow and apologize to trees before cutting them down.

No matter what its external appearance, then, the traditional Oriental house is therefore a complex and fascinating structure, both physically and conceptually. It expresses the ideals, aspirations and profound beliefs of the local society; it is conceived as being little more than a temporary shelter, yet it is the physical site and spiritual focus for the vital sense of cultural continuity from one generation to the next.

The 'curtain-walling' of the exterior of the house **(above)** allows the inhabitants protection against the volatile extremes of climate, but also affords vital ventilation during the summer months as the structure can be stripped down to an open-sided pavilion. The deliberate cultivation of vegetation enhances the sense of blurred boundaries between the house and the outside environment.

The *tokonoma*, or traditional alcove of Japanese architecture, provides a focal point for aesthetic expression in the interior **(above)**. Objects for contemplation, such as hanging scrolls or *ikebana* flower arrangements are carefully chosen to enhance what might otherwise be a somewhat austere setting. Although not conforming to the time-honoured *tatami* mat module, as found in the traditional house, the *tokonoma* still fulfils an essential rôle in a modern house in Beppu **(opposite)**; here the emphasis upon natural, unadorned materials is even more evident in the choice of bamboo trunks as the *higashi-daira*, or main pillar, of the recess.

The exterior of the contemporary Beppu house (left) uses bamboo as a decorative medium, and the entrance is masked by naturalistic shrubbery; the parallels are obvious when comparing this structure with a more orthodox modern house in Machida **(top)** and a traditional façade in Kyoto **(above)**.

A quintessentially traditional Japanese approach dictated the creation of this tea ceremony complex; in fact, these settings are located in a converted stable block in the centre of Manhattan.

In the traditional Oriental dwelling, the floor area is the social forum and, as such, it is deliberately kept as uncluttered as possible so that the available space may be maximized for domestic activities or when receiving visitors. The raised entrance porch of a rural Thai house **(left above)** is laid out with seating mats and low tables, in expectation of guests, while the formal reception room of a nineteenth-century Korean manor house **(left below)** similarly features low-level seating and provision for a group of visitors. The open-plan arrangement of Japanese homes is the epitome of versatility; the dividing *fusuma* screens can be removed from their running grooves to open the interior completely **(opposite)**.

ORIENTAL STYLES EAST AND WEST

The style of the Far East is a fascinating mélange of motifs and forms; high-tech sophistication more in keeping with Western expectations sits alongside indigenous forms and motifs. The neon lights of Hong Kong and the New Internationalism of massive skyscraper blocks confound the would-be Oriental purist who clings to the opulence of Chinese moulded ceilings and the rigorous simplicity of the Japanese bath-house. The peoples of the Orient keep a foot in each camp – as does this Paris apartment **(opposite)** which joyfully blends objects from East and West.

Part of the appeal of the best of traditional Far Eastern housing is undoubtedly the sense of harmony and tranquility which can apparently be derived from such a lifestyle. However, this universal dream is becoming steadily less attainable for the majority of the world's population. Since the beginnings of the Industrial Revolution in the West, cities have become increasingly congested and living space is consequently at a premium. Before the advent of mass transportation systems, it was imperative for workers to live within walking distance of their place of work; as a result, cities such as Paris, New York and London still contain enclaves of small-scale housing, while the coming of the railways created the option for the wealthier of living in the leafier suburbs, a pseudo-pastoral alternative for those who could afford the higher cost of land and the time and money required for daily commuting.

Nowadays, as public transportation systems are stretched to breaking point and the cost of living in the suburbs becomes impossible for many, the considerable potential of smaller city dwellings is being reassessed. The idea of inhabiting a studio flat or small apartment is still regarded with misgivings by many Westerners, because our upbringing leads us to demand plenty of space. Not only does this enable us to be away from our family and neighbours, it also enforces our sense of singularity and uniqueness. However, even if we are fortunate enough to acquire a territorial 'patch', we choose to define it by filling it with our belongings, all the impedimenta of everyday life which we feel are vital to our enjoyment, self-esteem and well-being.

Some of the world's most populous cities are those in the Far East; with the rapid expansion of the Pacific Basin and south-east Asia as a major industrial and economic forum, the ratio of living space to each human being in Hong Kong, Tokyo, Shanghai or Seoul has contracted to the point where it defies Western comprehension. Kowloon has the unenviable title of most densely-packed residential area in the world; the traffic jams of Bangkok are notorious and the sight of three million Japanese commuters flooding through Tokyo's Shinjuku station every rush hour is beyond description. Yet social anarchy does not erupt; the inner-city rioting and looting which sporadically breaks out in Western capitals and is so often attributed to overcrowding and the paucity of suitable housing does not seem to be a catalyst for freelance mayhem in Oriental cities. Inevitably, the struggle for space in Western cities will become more difficult in the next century, and given our lack of ability to tolerate what we feel to be constriction, it is time to analyze and evaluate the successful pragmatism of the Oriental approach to city dwelling.

The single, most profound difference between Western and Far Eastern approaches to what constitutes a home lies in the notion of neutral rather than specific definition of the different areas of the house. Traditionally, Westerners have grown up with the nineteenth-century notion of each room having a clearly-stated purpose and function. Consequently, we move constantly from one room to another, according to our activities. As a result, the remaining, uninhabited rooms are 'dead space'; while we eat in the dining room, the living room is unused, yet modern architects and builders reflect the desires of their clients by subdividing an already restricted space into tiny rooms to meet those expectations.

In order to further differentiate between the numerous, microcosmic environments we create for ourselves, we reinforce the sense of fragmentation by deliberately choosing particular colour schemes for each room, and revel in the fact that each room contrasts with the one adjacent to it. Furthermore, we limit our use of each room by cramming it with unwieldy furniture whose singular function is almost perversely enjoyed. The typical Western bedroom in a city apartment, for example, is usually small; we spend about one third of our lives in bed, yet by packing that room with a large, immobile bed, free-standing wardrobe, dressing tables, bedside tables and other articles, we deliberately restrict the potential for exploiting that space during the other sixteen hours of the day.

Perhaps the only exception to this rule is the Western living room, in which we gather to socialize, entertain visitors, watch television or otherwise amuse ourselves. In the Far East, virtually every room, with the obvious exceptions of the kitchen and bathroom, is considered to be a 'living room' - and dining room, and study, and bedroom. . . .

Traditional Oriental thinking discriminates against the inclusion of large, heavy pieces of furniture, particularly in a confined space, and especially if the items do not easily lend themselves to a variety of uses, including dismantling and storing with little effort. Although it has become fashionable among the wealthy in the Far East to have at least one overtly Western-style lounge (chiefly for entertaining), for most of the population the idea of purchasing a three-piece suite has little appeal. The initial cost is one consideration, but also there is the factor of its lack of applications, beyond the sole provision of a reasonably comfortable surface to sit on. Furthermore, a Western-style sofa generally defies even the most strenuous efforts to dismantle, fold or store it.

Most Oriental furniture intended for the home market is deliberately designed and purchased for its adaptability and ease of use. Modern Chinese, Korean or Japanese furniture for city dwellers is lightweight and portable; simple chairs fold and stack when not required, and much of the social life of the household is still conducted sitting on cushions, mats or small stools grouped around a low-level table. Chinese stacking tables nest one within the other when not in use, while the Japanese favour the *kotatsu*, especially in the winter months. The *kotatsu* looks like a coffee table, but is heated from underneath by an electrical element. The table top lifts out and is placed over a large padded quilt, so that family members can sit with their legs under the table to eat, talk, study, play games or watch television. The *kotatsu* is practical, space-saving and convivial; when not needed as an energy-saving source of heating during the summer, it can be used as an ordinary table or work-surface, or folded and stored.

The idea of portable bedding along Oriental lines has gained a growing number of Western converts. Dwellers in small apartments in major cities have welcomed an easy,

Hallways introduce the ambience of the interior – they are difficult places to decorate adequately, but should provide a hint of the nature of the rest of the setting. Two contrasting approaches are evident here. A brightly lit, severely minimalist, and rather rugged entrance hall to offices along Japanese modernist lines suggests an efficient, practical environment. The monochrome lattice-textured wallpaper of the hall of a London apartment **(opposite)** provides the perfect backdrop to the sinuous, sensual forms of Chinese rosewood furniture and fine antique ceramics, creating a softer, more intimate mood.

functional and inexpensive alternative to the grim morning ritual of grappling with a recalcitrant pile of sheets and blankets in order to reconstruct the sofa-bed. The *futon* is a flat, flexible mattress with a removable, washable cotton cover, and is used with a padded quilt, rather like a duvet. Both can be quickly folded and can serve the function of providing a seat during daytime, or can be stored in a cupboard. The advantages of the *futon* are that it can be laid out on any available floor, yet when not needed it does not occupy 'dead space'. As a practical solution to the perennial problem of providing a spare bed for guests, one Western company is now marketing a basic, single size *futon* which fits into its own duffel bag.

The key to living in this simpler, less cluttered way, is the absolute necessity of adequate, easy access storage; one can keep furniture to a basic, functional minimum, yet provision has to be made for all the belongings and domestic artefacts of the household. City apartments in the Far East tend to maximize the limited space available by containing built-in, floor-to-ceiling banks of cupboards and closets, rather than relying on Western-style individual chests, trunks, dressers or wardrobes. Ease of access and the more efficient use of floor space is often facilitated by the provision of double sliding doors to these cupboards. Therefore, any item superfluous to immediate requirements can be temporarily stored, but is instantly retrievable when needed.

The use of sliding doors as room dividers is a typically traditional feature of Oriental domestic life, but in recent years it has also proved to be invaluable in the rather more confined quarters of city apartments. Conventional side-hinged doors in the Western style tend to be narrow, yet require a clearance of at least the quarter-circle described by the edge of the door as it opens outwards. Double sliding panels need far less space, yet can also be easily removed from their running tracks so that two separate rooms can be opened into one; this device is also an efficient method of allowing the inhabitants to enjoy better ventilation during the humid summer months.

The traditional use of the module throughout the Far East has already been mentioned, both as an ergonomic principle and as a universally applicable set of standard measurements, but it is interesting to note how much of modern Oriental product design intended for a domestic setting has also benefitted from this principle. As an example, early Western hi-fi and stereo systems were large and rather rambling pieces of equipment, which were frequently designed to mimic the appearance of 'serious' furniture. They were rapidly superseded by the more compact 'tower' systems produced in the Far East; the amount of floor space or supporting furniture required is thus greatly reduced as the components are stacked vertically and are of uniform horizontal dimensions, rather like the traditional stacking food boxes and baskets found throughout the Far East. Similarly, the Oriental trend towards miniaturization through producing ever-smaller units has been of major benefit to many cramped Western homes. It is possible that we are now facing the prospect of the further development of 'integral multi-entertainment consoles', a stacking system possibly incorporating a television, stereo system, video, CD player, tape deck, VDU and personal computer.

Multi-entertainment consoles apart, the effect of simplicity and neutrality in the city apartment of the Far East is achieved by a number of traditional factors. The lack of dominant room fixtures, such as the ubiquitous fireplace or oppressive, large pieces of furniture means that the modern Oriental room has no single, clearly defined focal point, but naturally this has the advantage of allowing a number of different orientations for the inhabitants, and consequently it is unusual for visitors to feel that they are sitting in the 'wrong' place. Given the traditions of hospitality prevalent throughout the countries of south-east Asia, the honoured guest is usually seated so that he or she is facing a carefully chosen but essentially portable or ephemeral focal point, such as a hanging scroll, an aesthetically pleasing *objet d'art* or a flower arrangement. The lack of fixed decoration serves two functions; firstly, it allows constant change and rotation of decorative artefacts, and secondly it avoids both clutter and ostentation.

Subtlety and neutrality are also essential to the choice of colour schemes and wall coverings, which tend to be light in tone and gently textured rather than floridly patterned in order not to confuse the eye and so that light can be reflected, which enhances the sense of space. Natural light is often at a premium in the densely packed cities of the Far East, but it is frequently available only to the fortunate; building regulations in Tokyo stipulate that any new building must allow a mere two hours of natural light per day to the windows of neighbouring structures. Consequently, ingenious methods of mimicking natural sources of light are becoming popular and a recent innovation is the use of 'daylight' bulbs behind translucent screens or fake roller blinds, which in turn mask a blank wall.

While neutral colour schemes and built-in storage undoubtedly contribute to a sense of space and openness, it would not be accurate to claim that all indigenous Oriental interiors conform to this principle. As in other cultures, peoples of the Far East like to surround themselves with things that they believe to be beautiful, as well as those they know to be useful. In recent years, Oriental city dwellers have tended to opt for a more international blend of styles, and they are more likely to use stronger colour schemes, but they frequently retain their traditional approach to coping with the practical problems associated with living in a small space. Decoration is often provided by carefully-selected examples of their own country's arts and crafts, and antique collecting, particularly in the fields of architectural detailing, ceramics and paintings, is extremely popular in the Far East.

Completely Oriental style buildings are still comparatively rare in the West, so this example in Paris is remarkable for its uncompromising promulgation of traditional Chinese style. The interior is a sequence of rooms whose windows are barred with decorative lattice work **(right above and below)**, and the wooden furniture is low-level and features *kang* style – inwardly-curving – legs. The moon-shaped opening between one public room and another is a form commonly found in garden and external wall construction in pre-revolutionary Chinese buildings, but here it facilitates movement between the two spaces. The interior **(opposite)** is handsomely panelled in rich, dark wood; the pierced transoms allow ventilation while impressing the visitor with their understated opulence. The exterior of the building **(opposite lower right)** is roofed with flying gables in classical Chinese style, and the approach to the entrance is defined by a traditional roofed gateway; the encircled Chinese character signifies long life and prosperity.

Vibrant Eastern colour schemes can create a unique and personal version of Oriental style in the interiors of Western apartments and houses. The use of lacquered furniture and panelling in traditional shades of cinnabar red and black in these three interiors evokes an attractively warm and inviting atmosphere; it also provides a suitably unifying backdrop or visual counterpoint to the wide variety of Far Eastern art objects displayed. Two Japanese *noh* masks are placed against a Chinese painting **(above left)** and flanked by a Chinese lacquered cabinet. Another view of the same apartment **(below left)** shows the owner's collection of framed Chinese paintings against a custom-made red lacquer wall-panel, a successful stylistic hybrid which combines the traditional colours of China with rectilinear grid motifs derived from Japanese *shoji*. The Chinese table in the foreground is modern, while the gold-coloured blooms are Japanese.

This bedroom (opposite) in a London town house is presided over by a carving of a Chinese sage housed in an alcove above a Japanese trousseau trunk. Although the room is small, the location of an antique wooden carving and a Chinese lacquered panel at this height provides the valuable illusion of space. The overtly Chinese theme is reiterated in the opulent colour scheme and the lustrous sheen of the rich, subdued tones of the decorative lacquer panel, contributing to the ambience of exotic, sensuous luxury.

The decoration of bathrooms presents a wonderful opportunity for the application of Oriental style. High summer temperatures in this Andalusian house **(left)** dictated the use of marble, whose coolness of colour and touch makes it the ideal material. However, the understated classicism of the stone is enlivened by the antique Burmese gable end mounted on the wall, and a carved wooden panel inset on one fascia of the bath surround. The superb sculptural qualities of these pieces provide vital focal points in this otherwise simple, almost minimalist room.

The bathroom of a small London house (opposite) deliberately evokes an atmosphere of seductive luxury; strings of miscellaneous small objects, beads and carvings collected throughout the Far East are suspended over the bath to entertain the eye, and Thai and Burmese lacquered receptacles contain larger pieces of Oriental jewellery. A richly resonant colour scheme further adds to the impression of sensuousness and opulence.

An exquisite and intricate Tibetan devotional picture
(*thanka*) adorns the wall of a bedroom in a large country house, and
handwoven woollen rugs from the Far East cover the floors. The
asymmetrical shapes and fascias of two antique Japanese *tansu* chests
have a quietly resonant charm as well as providing ample storage space
and a broad, low-level surface for the display of favourite objects.

Simple Thai furniture makes an attractive and practical addition to this terrace overlooking a range of hills in southern Spain. The uncomplicated forms of the bamboo day beds and parasol, also from Thailand, look completely at home in a setting of rough stonework and terracotta tiles. The upholstery of the beds is covered in a sturdy *Ikat* material from north-east Thailand. An ornamental palm provides a dramatic centrepiece for the whole arrangement.

The understandable desire to cultivate greenery and to feel in touch with natural phenomena is a universal problem of city-dwellers the world over; Oriental peoples cope with this need by cultivating small-scale houseplants, *bonsai* trees or complete interior gardens in miniature inside their own homes. High-rise city blocks in the Far East nearly always have a small balcony to each apartment; while Westerners would use such a space to acquire a sun tan, Oriental balconies often house the washing machine, cunningly camouflaged from the viewpoint of the visitor by a plethora of carefully cultivated foliage. This concept is a natural development from the traditional practice of using the verandah as a workplace, and blurring the boundaries of the dwelling by bringing natural forms into the interior. The balcony is also the natural domain of the family pets, terrapins in aquaria, crickets in intricate wicker cages or chattering songbirds to bring a touch of nature to an otherwise unreservedly urban setting.

Much of the riotous colour and intricate detailing so typical of the Far East can be incorporated into Western apartments to great effect. The small scale and exquisite decoration of lacquerwork, textiles and miniature carvings make them particularly suited to use in restricted spaces. Those colours and finishes most often associated with the decorative arts of the Orient, such as brilliant embroidered silks, glossy lacquerware, cinnabar red, black and gold, can be successfully utilized as the colour scheme for small Western apartments; if used with conviction, they can bring an impression of exotic luxury and richness to an otherwise colourless interior.

In essence, the Oriental approach to modern city dwelling is one of adoption and adaptation, a blend of traditional modes of living with a pragmatic ability to make the most out of what seems to be unpromising. It could be argued that Far Eastern lifestyles have little in common with those of the West, not least in the cultural and religious conditioning which demands harmonious and non-confrontational co-existence with relatives and neighbours. It would certainly require a massive leap in Western social mores for the average extended family of Europeans or Americans to be able to live peacefully under the same conditions, and it would be foolish to recommend such a course.

However, as the global population shows no signs of shrinking or even remaining static, cities are becoming more congested and space is ever more restricted. Urban Chinese, Korean and Japanese families are gradually drawing closer in lifestyle to their Western counterparts – social aspirations, working practices and leisure pursuits are becoming more similar in East and West. The people of the Far East are able to adopt and adapt Occidental lifestyles, grafting them onto their traditional practices; it is also imperative that urban Westerners reassess their preconceptions of city life and are prepared to consider Oriental alternatives.

We should, perhaps, return for a moment to the role of colour in the evocation of Oriental styles in Western interiors. As we have noted above, the underlying tones of an Oriental interior frequently tend to be modulated and almost neutral; the ambience of the interior is created essentially by the interplay of light and 'natural' materials such as wood, textiles and even paper. In many of the interiors illustrated in this chapter, the most successful effects are achieved by the display of colourful or intricately shaped objects and furniture against such a background. Other rooms within the same apartment or house, however, may explore the opposite end of the Oriental palette – the reds, blacks and golds. Again, it is the appropriateness of the artefacts which are set against these more assertive backgrounds which ensures the degree of success of the whole setting.

What is remarkable in all the interiors illustrated here is the evidence of total attention to detail. It is one thing to arrange heavier pieces of furniture pleasingly, it is quite another to finish an interior with a complementary display of other types of object. Fortunately, though, the decorative arts of the Orient are especially rich in artefacts which have a high and dramatic 'display' value, and we shall devote a later chapter entirely to the effective arrangement of decorative objects. In the meantime, the interiors here will repay careful analysis of their owners' ability to evoke dramatic and entirely Oriental effects through the combination of colour, light and object, from Japanese screens to Thai tables and Burmese lacquerware.

In conclusion, it is worth noting how some of the illustrations in this chapter bring into focus the profound influence which the more minimalist aspects of Oriental, especially Japanese, design have had on Western interior designers and architects. A number of Modernist European designs illustrated here show a simplicity of colour scheme allied to an ingenious organization of space which is drawn directly from the traditional Oriental dwelling. In the same vein, the Orientophile and would-be interior decorator may reflect on how well certain works by Modernist Western furniture designers – notably Le Corbusier and Eileen Gray – seem entirely at home in a simply conceived Oriental setting.

Low-level tables are an integral part of Oriental life, and can be successfully used in Western settings as an ideal surface for the display of decorative objects. Examples of such tables can be seen in these three interiors **(right)**, including a particularly fine antique table from Thailand **(above)**, a Japanese table inlaid with mother-of-pearl **(centre)** and one from Indonesia **(below)**. It is interesting to note that in all these interiors, not only are the objects of Far Eastern origin, but they are also arranged in a way which owes a great deal to traditional Oriental practice. In one case, an exquisite gold screen **(opposite)** provides a backdrop to the central focal point of the table, and plants or flower arrangements break up the harder edges of the furniture.

In a London apartment, the problem of creating a balustrade to protect the stairwell without enclosing it has been successfully solved by the use of traditional wooden Chinese window screens. The effect is light, airy and decorative.

The inspiration for this practical storage scheme in the entrance to a small apartment is entirely Oriental; the Japanese store anything superfluous, while eight (there are eight doors) is a lucky number for the Chinese. The two central doors open on to a kitchen, and the right-hand pair lead to the hall, while others house books and household necessities. The alcoves contain rocks from China.

The owner of this New York apartment successfully employed an Oriental approach to the interior design of her home, and the result is a pleasing, harmonious combination of objects and artefacts drawn from a number of Far Eastern countries. The dark colours and rich surfaces of Oriental furniture can appear heavy and oppressive if cluttered and jammed together; in this living room each piece seems to sit comfortably with its neighbours. The antique wooden chest from Tibet in the living room **(opposite)** is painted with exquisite scenes, imbued with the subtle patina of age. The geometric design of the original parquet floor is accentuated by the diagonal pattern of the handwoven Tibetan rug, but the harder lines are alleviated by Chinese touches; the scroll-mounted ancestor painting and the statues soften the angles, while an unusual display of flowers in a Japanese basket breaks the rectilinear theme.

Across the room, a particularly fine Chinese table in yuna wood is flanked by traditional rosewood armchairs **(right above)**, providing a suitable foil for the curved, elegant forms of the Ming horse and statue of Buddha. Similarly, an important piece of statuary is silhouetted against the window **(right below)**; the sinuous lines of the Javanese deer combine with the abstract patterns of the Tibetan tiger rug to provide movement and texture in this well-chosen and unobtrusive Oriental scheme.

A minimalist city apartment designed by an architect with a deep affinity for and knowledge of the minimalism of Japan, both traditional and modern. The silhouette of the stairwell **(opposite above left)** recalls the form of the traditional *kaidan-dansu*, or below-stairs storage chest, while the unadorned natural materials of the interiors and overtly structural elements are a fascinating blend of modernist and traditional themes. The remarkable interplay of different levels adds to the sense of interpenetrating space **(opposite above right and right)**; the installation of a portable wooden screen **(opposite below)** introduces an element of adaptability to the room.

In a small London apartment, the challenge of making the most of a limited space has been successfully met by adopting a traditional Japanese approach; an illusion of ample space is created by blending the best of East and West. The work and leisure areas of the living room (**top**) are recessed in the fashion of a *tokonoma* (traditional meditational recess), and the bookshelves are stepped in the manner of *chigai-dana*, or 'broken mist' shelves. Translucent screens allow ample light without distracting the inhabitants, and the floor area is left uncluttered and simple.

Sliding *fusuma* (screens) divide the living room from the bedroom, which is a masterpiece in Japanese-style understatement (**left and opposite below**). Wooden structural elements remain unpainted and unadorned, relying for their visual impact on the beauty of the natural wood grain. The resulting rectilinear scheme is echoed in the geometric pattern of the futon cover. Air and light circulate through the *ramma* or grille between ceiling and room dividers, and built-in closets discreetly conceal the impedimenta of everyday life.

The kitchen of this apartment (**above**) is the room which is the least overtly Japanese in style, yet it retains many of the essential characteristics of modern Oriental city dwelling. The grid effect of *shoji* over the window is repeated in the rectilinear format of the bank of built-in storage units, while the continuous bench of working surface on the opposite wall allows a small space to be effectively used by the occupants. Lightweight stools tuck under the counter when not required, and the result is a pleasant and efficient working environment.

Although modern Japanese sometimes adopt Western seating in their own homes **(left)**, nevertheless they still favour the simplicity of the past. An almost empty room (by Western standards) is adorned only by a hanging scroll in the *tokonoma*, or recess **(below)**.

Each *tatami* floor mat measures 6 feet by 3 feet, and the universal use of this traditional module dictates the shape and dimensions of the interior **(above and opposite)**; indeed, the size of a Japanese house is described by the number of mats it contains, rather than the number of individual rooms. Simple, translucent screens filter light **(left)** to emphasize the calm of the rooms.

**Both the closet space and *tokonoma* recess
(above)** conform to the dimensions of *tatami* mats;
cupboard doors and *fusuma* interior partitions can
be opened to maximize the floor space.

Natural light streams through the *shoji*, the sliding window frames covered in translucent rice paper; the grid motif echoes the geometric scheme so typical of traditional Japanese rooms.

The emphasis upon the exposed pillar and beam construction of the traditional Japanese dwelling **(left)** is particularly apparent in this house in Kyoto, and the interplay of timbers and articulated, interpenetrating space bears more than a passing resemblance to the Mackintosh Library in Glasgow (see p.15). Carefully selected *tansu* chests and ceramic pieces are highlighted by their considered location in relation to the regular geometric division of the wall surfaces **(opposite)**.

The rich colours and exotic forms of Oriental furniture and objects make an exciting and dramatic display against the neutral background of this living room in a London town house. Particularly striking are the lacquered bowls from Thailand and the hanging textile from Indonesia. The table and the chair on the right are both antique Thai pieces which combine easily with the modern Italian leather sofa.

The combination of modern European and traditional Oriental design is continued in the bedroom of the same house. The minimalist form of an angled 'Tizio' lamp nicely complements the opulence of an Indonesian bed cover, while the simplicity and ingenuity of much Oriental design is present in the form of the Chinese lacquered baskets to the left of the photograph.

Just a few miles north of Rome, this modern Italian house consists of a series of interrelated spaces suggestive of the traditional Oriental dwelling. It is appropriate therefore that most of the decorative objects in the sitting and dining areas **(left and above)** are from Thailand, Cambodia and Laos. This extensive open space on the ground floor is notable for its decorative use of statuary and other objects, creating a lively and uncluttered effect; especially impressive is the cylindrical form of a Thai ceremonial drum.

This English country house has been
refurnished using a collection of fascinating and
unusual Oriental pieces, particularly from Tibet
(above). The serpentine forms of a set of antique
Chinese furniture are the spectacular focal points of
the living room **(right)**.

The powerful religious iconography and symbolism of the Orient abounds in these two interiors; particularly fine Tibetan *thankas* are displayed on the walls, while the rug features a design incorporating the swastika, an ancient Hindu symbol meaning eternal life, which is also found throughout China, Tibet and Japan.

Behind the façade of this house in the centre of Paris lies a series of interiors furnished almost entirely in the Oriental style. The morning room **(opposite)** is an essay in late nineteenth-century Chinese style, from the delicate bamboo furniture to the elegant pattern of the carpet which, although suggestive of a place of manufacture such as Beijing or Shanghai, is in fact Portuguese.

The décor of the small sitting room **(left above)** is notable for its panels of painted silk (in the Oriental style by a French painter), a superb bronze animal sculpture from China, and *tabourets* from Hong Kong. The combination of decorative elements is continued in the library **(left below)**.

The interpenetration of the house and surrounding vegetation is an essential characteristic of traditional Oriental homes; the view from the patio of a Bangkok living room is of abundant foliage, softening the harder lines of the structure. The effect of a room opening out on to a profusion of tropical foliage and decorative pots is repeated in a Western-style sitting room, from which sliding doors lead into an intimate town garden **(inset)**.

Plants, shrubs and trees in a Bangkok garden are deliberately cultivated close to the series of connected buildings which constitute the traditional home **(opposite)**. The proximity of such abundant foliage emphasizes the symbiotic relationship between man and his environment which is so integral to Thai Buddhism; amidst the profusion of vegetation, man-made objects such as statues or wooden drums **(right)** epitomize this interdependence. It is also considered fortuitous for the future prosperity and happiness of the family to encourage natural forms in and around the dwelling, as these are believed to harbour animistic spirits whose patronage and support can help the inhabitants.

The inspiration for this restful, harmonious apartment (above and opposite) is entirely Japanese in its free-flowing space, strong vertical divisions, sliding room dividers and miniature bamboo grove. However, it also incorporates European Modernist design classics, such as armchairs by Le Corbusier **(below left)** to create a highly successful fusion of the best of East and West.

The traditional Japanese garden (right and opposite) is designed and cultivated to be viewed ideally from within the house, preferably from a seated vantage point on a *tatami* mat or verandah just beyond the *shoji*. The layout is intended to provoke not only visual interest but also a profounder sense of satisfaction derived from contemplation, through a symbolic re-creation of nature in microcosm. In order to heighten the sense of limitless distance, an interesting *trompe l'oeil* technique is occasionally used in smaller gardens; large-leaved plants are placed close to the house, while smaller-leaved shrubs and bushes are located at the outer edges of the vista, thus making the boundaries seem further from us than they actually are.

A series of minimalist interiors by a contemporary British architect who has a strong affinity with both the traditions of Japanese architecture and the current reinterpretations of those fundamental principles. Textured plastered surfaces are juxtaposed with the flawless finish of a stainless steel washbasin (converted from a food mixing bowl), simple balcony safety rails **(opposite)** and a folded metal staircase reminiscent of *origami* folded paper **(below left)**.

FURNITURE AND FURNISHINGS

The continuous Western fascination with the Far East and the recurring fashions for objects from Asia makes it hardly surprising that a great deal of Oriental furniture, both antique and modern, can be found in the West. What is less well-known, however, is the traditional lack of numerous, weighty pieces in standard Oriental homes. Consequently, for several centuries, Far Eastern merchants and manufacturers have catered for foreign demand by recreating pieces more commonly found in palaces or temples, rather than in domestic settings. Similarly, the designs, materials and decorative processes used by furniture-makers rely substantially on past practices; indeed, the forms of much contemporary furniture from the Far East can be considered to be Asian 'design classics'. Whether antique or modern, Oriental furniture and furnishings generally show high standards of craftsmanship, a genuine respect for their raw materials, and a highly-developed aesthetic sense.

In any setting, furniture and furnishings fulfil a predominantly practical purpose; we require working surfaces at an optimum height, places to store or display our possessions, and comfortable support for our bodies while asleep or resting. Ideally, these pieces should be functional and easy to clean and care for, but they are also the backdrop against which we live our lives. Therefore they play an important psychological role in providing us with visual pleasure and enjoyment while, almost incidentally, stating our view of ourselves as we would like others to see us. Assuming that there is an element of choice in the nature and form of our surroundings, it is vital that serious thought is given to the careful selection of those items which will enhance the quality of our lives. The Japanese concept of *mono no aware*, 'to understand and respond to the appeal of objects to the human heart', is one aspect of the general Oriental approach to aesthetics; in the case of furniture and furnishings, it is also the key to creating an Oriental-style interior which is both functional and attractive.

Despite the rapid industrialization of much of the Far East in recent times, the values and practices of the craft traditions are still respected and upheld. Indeed, in many countries within the region, there has been a resurgence of interest in native culture, and government support has been forthcoming in preserving and encouraging traditional skills. Both Korea and Japan honour certain master craftsmen, such as weavers, lacquer-makers or carvers, as 'National Living Treasures', because of their recognized supremacy and depth of knowledge in their chosen fields. Such individuals are regarded as highly competent professionals and not only is their social status high, but they also benefit from the lack of distinction traditionally found throughout the region between what Westerners classify as the 'fine arts', 'the applied arts' and 'crafts'. As a result, these 'masters' are able to pass on their considerable expertise in the time-honoured methods of production to younger family members and their apprentices.

Naturally, the objects produced under such exacting, labour-intensive conditions are much sought after and very expensive, but the sense of veneration for the old which is so much a part of the contemporary Far East still dictates the forms of much of the furniture and furnishings which are produced, using more modern technology at far lower costs. The manufactories of Korea and Thailand and the small co-operatives of China produce and export relatively inexpensive pieces of furniture made according to wholly traditional designs; production methods may have advanced but, stylistically speaking, the forms, motifs and materials are timeless classics – indeed, part of their desirability for Westerners lies in their ageless appeal, which contrasts so greatly with our own efforts to keep up with the cycle of constantly changing fashions.

A large variety of different materials have been used in furniture throughout the Orient but, as in the selection of building components for the traditional house, the choice of raw materials for the majority of domestic furniture was dependent upon their local availability. It is often (though not always) the case that locally grown woods are those most suited to the vicissitudes of particular climates. Hence, the timber traditionally used for furniture is likely to be native to that area, so that teak and rosewood furniture is considered to be typical of Thailand, Malaysian pieces are often mahogany, and varieties of cypress form the carcasses of many Japanese pieces. However, as in all cultures, there is a certain cachet attached to the exotic and the unusual, and Far Eastern craftsmen have avidly sought rare and costly woods, stones or mother-of-pearl to use as decorative inlays on small, intricate pieces for the luxury markets. Scented woods, such as sandalwood, cypress or camphor, have long been favourite materials among Oriental cabinet-makers for trunks and storage chests intended for textiles, partly because the aroma deters the attentions of moths.

A late nineteenth-century parquetry bureau, made in Japan for export.

Perhaps the best known of all Oriental materials for furniture is lacquer, which is known as *ch'i shu* in China, the country in which it was first discovered and developed. By the sixth century A.D., knowledge of the lacquering process had spread to Korea and then to Japan – both countries were quick to exploit this versatile and attractive new material, as it combines lightness of weight with subtlety and depth of colour, yet it is surprisingly resilient. The *rhus vernicifera* tree, the sap of which forms the basis of lacquer, is widespread across Asia, and trees of around fifteen years old are customarily considered to produce the best-quality sap. Tapping takes place during the summer months: horizontal slashes are made in the bark, and the collected liquid is boiled and filtered to remove impurities. The resin is tinted where necessary, using cinnabar to give a red hue, iron filings to turn the substance black, or orpiment (yellow sulphide of arsenic) to achieve a golden yellow. Traditional Chinese lacquer-makers also extended the colour range to include crimson, vermilion, and olive green.

Lacquer can be applied to almost any material (including fabric, bronze, porcelain and basketware) because of its powerful adhesive qualities. However, in the case of furniture, soft pinewood is the preferred base, although some modern Chinese lacquer has a chipboard skeleton. Individual hard-wood components are thoroughly shaped and smoothed before being coated in lacquer with a spatula or brush. After each application, a lengthy drying period is needed in a dust-free, damp environment – some modern Japanese lacquermakers dry their wares on boats on lakes. Once dry, the surface is polished and re-coated. A high quality piece of lacquer is often the result of thirty individual coats, and it is the gradual build-up of depth that gives the material its deep lustre and sheen. Once the components of the piece have been assembled, further applications of lacquer may be used to cover the joints, or alternatively the junctures may be bound with brass or iron to mask the connection and also to reinforce the edges for protection agnst accidental damage.

Although strictly speaking, the colour range of lacquer is limited to the tones mentioned above, the variety of decoration used on lacquer furniture is extensive. Semi-precious stones or jade were often applied to the surface of Chinese screens and decorative panels. Lacquer can also be carved into intricate designs and, in mainland China, Korea and Taiwan, the

The traditional wooden Japanese *kaidan-dansu* storage chest fits under a staircase, providing valuable extra space. The geometric theme continues in the set of lacquered, tiered boxes from Thailand, and in the chequerboard design of a Tibetan rug.

The angles created by a Chinese screen break up the wall space and provide a perfect backdrop to the Boddhisatva statue. Similarly, a Japanese woven basket on the chest and the use of plants add texture to this rectilinear setting.

A Korean cabinet from the last century, inlaid with mother-of-pearl.

incised areas are often then painted in pastel colours or gold so that the pattern stands out against the darker background. Japanese lacquered pieces tend to be more subdued in design, but glossier in texture; before the final few coats are applied, gold and silver may be applied in a restrained traditional pattern. By contrast, it was undoubtedly the more ornately decorated mother-of-pearl inlaid black lacquered furniture so typical of south China that took the fancy of Westerners in the nineteenth century, and highly decorative and intricate pieces are still made there and in Vietnam. Lacquered furniture tended to be used in religious buildings, palaces and public meeting places – in both design and colour it was intended to impress.

The rich lustre and heavy colours of lacquerware may not suit all tastes and, for the would-be Oriental stylist, less ornate and expensive alternative furniture materials are readily available. In sub-tropical climates, such as Macao and Indonesia, woven cane and rattan furniture is ideally practical as it is lightweight and airy, while the natural fibres can easily withstand the heat and humidity. The frame or carcass of the piece is usually of some local wood to add strength to the structure and, as a design, its resistance to wear has been proven over centuries of use. The pattern of the weave is frequently traditional and often bears more than a passing resemblance to local textile designs, fretwork motifs or architectural elements. Earlier this century, Western traders and plantation owners in Malaysia and Singapore came to appreciate the advantages of locally-made cane and rattan furniture over their own well-upholstered plush suites brought from home, and although imports of chairs and settees to Europe and America were initially intended as garden or summerhouse furniture, their versatility and comfort led to their advance via the patio or verandah into the heart of the Western home. Cane and rattan furniture provides an economical, durable and surprisingly comfortable alternative, particularly when padded with cushions.

Bamboo used to be the most widespread Oriental raw material for furniture, but despite its remarkable strength, its quick-growing nature and its attractive appearance, it fell from favour in the West earlier this century, perhaps a victim of its own popularity and because it was inextricably if unfairly associated with the worst excesses of the high Victorian era. However, it is interesting to note the recent resurgence of interest in painting furniture and furnishings in *trompe l'oeil* effects to imitate other materials; enterprising interior designers and enthusiastic amateurs are now 'bambooing' pieces to mimic the appearance of the material. Hardwoods such as teak, rosewood and mahogany are becoming rarer as a result of attempts to preserve the natural forests of south-east Asia, and consequently it is likely that bamboo will return to favour as a versatile and easily replenishable raw material.

The forms of Oriental furniture are reflections of both the practical requirements and the aesthetic preferences of their owners, but they tend to share a common regard for quality of materials and skilled workmanship, no matter what their purpose or cultural origins. The two main characteristics of the traditional Far Eastern interior are the general absence of large, solid and unwieldy pieces of furniture, especially in a confined space, and the low-level design of many pieces, a feature which necessarily evolved from the customary habit of sitting, working and resting on the floor.

Seating Oriental-style can be a problem, as in certain societies Western-style chairs have only recently been adopted for everyday use. Much of the day-to-day business of traditional Asian family life is still conducted at floor level, a habit that has to be acquired in early years in order to accustom the body to this practice. However, less agile Westerners are not alone in finding squatting cross-legged or sitting on their heels uncomfortable; modern Japanese people, particularly office workers who spend their working hours in a Western-style environment, have taken to the *za-isu*, or 'legless chair', with alacrity and find the tilted seat and backrest to be the ideal compromise between tradition and comfort. A number of Western companies now manufacture this kind of chair for use in otherwise sparsely-furnished Oriental interiors.

The Japanese and Korean practice of sitting on the floor came originally from China, but by the second century A.D. both the armchair and the folding stool had gained some popularity among the wealthier Chinese, having been brought from India by Chinese traders. Chinese cabinet-makers began to create simple chairs in finely-grained aromatic woods; these were known as *hu ch'uang*, or 'barbarian couches'. No nails or screws were used by Chinese furniture makers, who relied upon their expertise in joinery to produce sturdy pieces which could also easily be knocked down and reassembled when required. Despite efforts to negate the values and forms of the past during the Cultural Revolution, contemporary Chinese furniture-making co-operatives have returned to producing thoroughly traditional styles of furniture for export, and rosewood or blackwood dining chairs and carvers make attractive additions to Orientalist interiors.

The traditional storage furniture of the Far East is the rectangular cabinet with front-opening doors and numerous small drawers. At its simplest, in rural China, the carcass was usually of a heavy wood, such as white fir or gingko. Typically, such Chinese cabinets were fitted with brass hinges, locking-plates and corner pieces to reinforce the structure and protect against accidental damage. Chests with many small drawers were used by traders or apothecaries to store their goods, and the contents were often labelled on the fascia of the chest in attractive Chinese characters. Modern reproductions of these designs are exported from Korea, and they make attractive, useful additions to Western settings.

For the storage of clothes or textiles, top-opening trunks with tightly-fitting lids were generally favoured throughout the region, and these pieces were often made from or lined with camphor wood to deter marauding insects. Trunks and small chests containing valuables can easily be moved to safety in the event of fire, and for this reason the *tansu* chest of Japan was particularly popular in provincial city homes where the rapid spread of fire from a neighbour's house was a constant threat. The fittings of the *tansu* are typically made of

Antique Korean medicine and scholars' chests (left above and below) provide useful storage for small items, and their rich, dark wood and chased brass fittings are extremely attractive. The decorative effect in these London living rooms is heightened by the balanced arrangement of Karen hill-tribe baskets from Thailand's Golden Triangle and Chinese 'double happiness' ceramics.

The sinuous sculptural form of a Lahu hill-tribe musical instrument **(opposite)** echoes the lines of the Breuer 'Wassily' chair. The small Japanese *kuruma-dansu* (wheeled chest) contrasts with the striking sofa covers and blinds of Thai silk – the result being a successful synthesis of East and West.

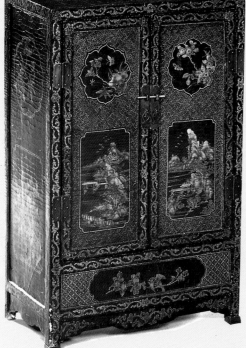

chasen iron, and the size varies according to the requirements of the original owner, from small-scale medicine chests to the large, rather portly pieces on wheels, known as *kuruma-dansu*. Less common but extremely useful is the *kaidan-dansu*, or 'staircase' chest which was designed and usually custom-made to fit under the stairs of a Japanese house. In a Western environment it can provide not only invaluable storage space, but also an intriguingly stepped profile on which to display favourite objects.

The folding screens of the Far East were among the most avidly collected imports during the early years of trade with the West, and they remain a favourite fixture in Orientalist interiors. As well as providing an instant decorative backdrop (and, incidentally, masking anything that should remain unseen), screens are also a practical way of dividing interior space and can be particularly useful in larger, open-plan Western settings such as converted lofts or warehouses. Contemporary examples are nearly always Chinese in origin, and are usually lacquered, but occasionally painted folding screens from Korea or Japan can be found in the West, although these tend to be very expensive and rather fragile.

By contrast, altar tables are ideally suited to the narrow hallways of many modern Western homes; tall and slim, the forms are elegant and fit beautifully into Western homes. In keeping with the best traditions of Chinese cabinet-making, the component pieces rely upon clever, exact joinery for the strength of the structure, rather than the reinforcement provided by nails or screws associated with Western models. Traditionally, altar tables were used for religious offerings, although they have adapted well to secular use. Southern China, especially the area around Nanjing, continues to be a major producer of stained hardwood chairs and tables, although the Thais have recently adopted Chinese designs and currently produce exquisite furniture in a variety of treated and bleached woods, which are light-coloured and have a slightly weather-beaten texture.

Of particular interest to Westerners is the size and attractiveness of square-topped Thai low tables, which usually have inwardly curved *kang*-style legs; not only do they make excellent coffee tables, but in the larger sizes they have been used as double bed bases. When used for this purpose, Thai tables are particularly impressive if combined with a piece of carving to form the bedhead.

Sleeping Oriental-style offers a number of different options, depending upon taste, space and finance. It is possible although rare to come across traditional Chinese marriage beds, known as *hua li*; ornately canopied four-posters with high sides, they are constructed to slot together without nails, and are sometimes made of delicately scented woods which are then usually painted or lacquered red, historically considered to be a fortuituous and fruitful colour in China. Marriage beds are also frequently adorned with carvings and motifs associated with monogamy and fidelity, such as cranes and ducks, in the hope that this will ensure the future stability, fertility and happiness of the honeymooners. Although fantastic and riotous pieces of furniture, Chinese marriage beds do have an opulent appeal all of their own.

From the simple to the ornate (opposite): a nineteenth-century Chinese rosewood display cabinet with an asymmetrical arrangement of shelves and a brass bar lock **(above)**, a Korean cabinet of similar period with numerous small drawers and brass bandings **(centre)**, and a Chinese lacquered cabinet intricately decorated in gold on a black ground **(below)**.

The increasing availability in the West of furniture and furnishing materials from the countries of the Far East has made possible the creation of whole Oriental interior schemes, using either eclectic arrangements drawing on a variety of national styles, or furniture from a single country. From the cheapest Chinese lacquered cardboard portmanteau, to the modestly priced Korean wedding chest, to the most exquisite Japanese screen, with mother-of-pearl inlay, Oriental furniture can now be found in the West at all price levels to fulfil every function in the home. The stylized lines of Chinese altar tables **(opposite and below)** provide perfect foils to the sculptural qualities of Chinese 'scholars' rocks' and other decorative objects.

Classic furniture designs from China, such as the stool and low table **(left below)**, have a timeless simplicity. The two pairs of elegant armchairs **(left and centre)** are over 250 years old, yet the folding armchair **(right)** is of modern southern Chinese manufacture, even though it conforms to a traditional design.

Traditional designs continue to be made for export markets, and sit well in many Western settings, such as the window bay of a country house **(right above)**. A lively and exuberant blend of old and new Oriental pieces **(right below)**; a Tibetan painting and low table supporting a Burmese lacquer bowl are offset by a contemporary classic design, the 'Wink' chair.

The wooden furniture of Indonesia is the result of a blend of influences, encompassing both a succession of European colonial styles and the continual, underlying reliance upon traditional zoomorphic or natural forms as stylistic motifs. Two impressive carver chairs with woven cane seats flank a table in an alcove of a London living-room **(below)**; despite their initially Western look, their Indonesian origins are revealed in the flowing, organic curves of the carcases, a theme reiterated in the anthropomorphic forms of a pair of Indonesian carvings which are used as tie-backs for the curtains, and in the use of a curvilinear animal sculpture as a focal point on the table-top.

In the same apartment (above), a weighty-looking wooden glass-fronted cabinet is used to display a collection of Oriental ceramics; the design of the chest and its decorative pediment is an unusual fusion of European Colonial and Chinese influences, but the quality of the craftsmanship and the materials used make it unmistakably Indonesian.

By contrast, the ultimate in portable, simple and unobtrusive bedding is the Japanese *futon*, a soft, padded mattress filled with cotton wadding which can be rolled and stored when not needed. The natural fibres of the filling material are particularly well-suited to people with allergies to Western-style mattresses and the *futon* provides an extremely comfortable night's sleep to those who require a firm base to correct a bad back. The *futon* should be aired regularly and turned occasionally to retain its springiness, and those who favour the purist approach can also buy the traditional Japanese *makuro* or small pillow, which is filled with dried beans. In Japan *futon* only come in single sizes, but Western manufacturers produce otherwise authentic versions in double sizes and longer lengths to suit Occidental frames.

Naturally, carpet- and rug-making in the Far East is largely confined to those countries which have a more severe climate. Northern China probably leads the field in this area, producing large quantities of modern mass-produced Chinese carpets for export. The designs are derived from traditional sources, frequently featuring plant, flower and wave formations, and the results are often extremely attractive, if somewhat stylized and usually available only in pastel colour schemes. It is possible to come across very fine antique Chinese rugs and carpets in silk or wool, but they tend to be extremely expensive as they were generally confined to aristocratic or religious settings. The dimensions of these types of carpet do not usually lend themselves easily to the majority of modern Western homes, as they were often made to be displayed on walls or wrapped around tall pillars in temples.

By contrast, the traditional woollen rugs and carpets of Tibet are smaller in scale and extremely adaptable; designs range from eyecatching geometric motifs to the stylized animal markings of 'tiger' prayer rugs, a popular pattern throughout the Far East because of the perception of the tiger as a symbol of strength and integrity. It is also possible to acquire rugs and carpets hand-made by Chinese minorities who live in the north of the country and are actively encouraged to produce their traditional woven carpets according to time-honoured designs, which are often colourful and highly attractive.

Middle Eastern traders and merchants called the arduous overland trek to the Orient 'The Silk Route' because of the consistent allure of that sumptuous fabric. The recent world shortage due to disease amongst silkworms has caused a massive escalation in the price of that material, and this situation has been compounded by the import quotas imposed by certain Western governments in an effort to protect their own textile manufacturers. The dazzling colours and exciting textures of Thai slubbed silks are exceptionally attractive, especially in the case of two-tone heavy-weight dupion, the iridescent lustre of which is achieved by weaving the warp in a contrasting colour to the weft. The prevailing Indian influence in Thailand has led to the production of delicately-coloured silk *ikats*, an exacting and methodical process whereby the filaments are pre-dyed at precise intervals so that when they are woven together, the juxtaposition of different colours creates a subtle and beautiful pattern. Although expensive in quantity, this lightweight fabric is ideally suited to making up into cushion covers, bedspreads or curtains.

China remains the main source of silk to the West, and the wide variety of weights and textures from that country is remarkable. The lightest weight of Chinese silk (excluding crêpe de chine or chiffon) is *habutai* silk, and this can be used to create filmy, lightweight drapes which are well suited to windows as a welcome alternative to net curtains, blinds, or similar screening devices. The most attractive Chinese silk is usually natural-coloured or white; the dyed colours of silk meterage from mainland China can be slightly flat and a little disappointing, although in recent years, Hong Kong textile merchants have bought up vast quantities of undyed Chinese silks and commissioned the dyeing locally to colour ranges more in accordance with Western tastes, before exporting them to the West.

One area of silk production in which China excels is in the production of ornate brocade, a highly decorative middleweight fabric which is eminently suitable for furnishings and upholstery which will only receive moderate wear. Northern China can be very dry and dusty during the summer, and this densely-woven fabric was traditionally made up into dust covers for valued objects; nowadays, it is widely used to cover the television set in modern Chinese homes. The designs of silk brocade are usually created by using the 'jacquard' technique, which means that the 'wrong' side carries the same pattern with reverse coloration, a feature which can be exploited to great effect in combining pieces from the same bolt. Chinese silk brocade tends to be highly decorative and luxurious in effect, as the 'right' side has a high lustre and the patterns used are very colourful, featuring traditional motifs, such as plum blossoms, roundels of calligraphic seals or seething dragons. Figured silk brocade would be ideal for coverings or cushions in a bedroom, particularly on a Chinese wedding bed and makes up well into dramatic curtains or hangings.

The traditionally-patterned cotton fabrics available in mainland China do not generally reach the West, yet they are among the most appealing, as interesting textures, designs and for their frequently exuberant colouring. Monochromatic cotton brocades, whose simple patterns and durability recommend them to Westerners are perfect for table-cloths and bed coverings, but the printed textiles are particularly exciting. It is possible to buy lengths featuring seething phoenixes or dragons against a predominantly red background, which are customarily used by families for celebrations, such as marriage or New Year festivities.

The embroidered textiles of northern China are similarly colourful and generally reach the West as piece goods, such as ready-made cushions or table-cloths. Although the infamous 'Peking stitch', an elaborate confection of tiny French knots, was outlawed by the government because of the deleterious effect it had on the eyes of the workers, the standard of needlework remains remarkable and largely unparalleled in the West.

The embroidered products of Hong Kong, Singapore and Taiwan tend to conform to the traditional designs associated with Chinese culture, and the 'white-on-white' embroidery is

Much of the contemporary manufacture of wooden furniture in China is based in the areas around Jiangsu and Shanghai, using imported hardwoods from a variety of sources. A pair of restrained modern Chinese chairs in traditional style flank a highly decorative side-table in a London apartment **(opposite)**, and a matching chair and desk set in a study decorated with Oriental artefacts offers a practical and highly attractive working environment **(right)**.

particularly attractive, especially when combined with intricate cut-work. It is possible to buy table linen and bedding of remarkable quality through Oriental emporia and larger department stores in most major Western cities.

The textiles of Japan are remarkably different, partly because, with the exception of the first three decades of this century, the Japanese tended to produce traditional textiles for domestic consumption only. Although the Japanese now export large quantities of polyester fabrics specifically designed for Western markets, their native textiles are still largely unavailable in the West. A wide variety of materials are still produced to meet the home demand for furnishing and dress fabrics. Of these, the best-known in the West is perhaps *mompe* or workwear, the indigo-dyed clothing traditionally worn by farmers, which enjoyed a recent craze amongst fashionable Westerners. *Mompe* is a cotton woven according to the *ikat* principle, so that small irregular patterns occur throughout the fabric. Indigo was favoured as a dyeing technique because it makes cotton up to ten per cent stronger, and because the slightly earthy smell it gives off is repellant to the poisonous snakes which live in the paddy fields of southern Japan.

The traditional blue-and-white printed heavyweight cotton of Japan is known as *kasuri*. It is eminently suitable for making up as upholstery fabric for settees or chairs, as it is usually used for the covers for *zabuton*, the native firm, square floor cushions, which make an attractive and practical seating alternative in minimalist Western interiors. The patterns of *kasuri* are either geometric or conventionalized plant and animal motifs, and in this respect they have a certain amount in common with the intricate designs of Indonesian or Balinese *batiks*. However, the methods of production vary considerably; *batik* is a highly-skilled, labour-intensive method of multi-dyeing cotton fabrics using the resistant properties of wax, and the best examples are resonantly colourful and subtle in effect. *Batik* material has long been available in the West, but recently the same technique has been used to create wall-hangings and piece goods of surprising quality, which are eagerly bought by Westerners to be made into window blinds, curtains or bedspreads.

Traditional Far Eastern garments also make extremely effective wall hangings in Western interiors. The quality of materials and workmanship, and the often rich, subtle coloration of such items makes them ideal focal points of decorative interest. Mandarin robes of pre-revolutionary China are most effectively displayed on tailor's dummies, as they tend to be very full at the hem, and this method allows the often intricate embroidery of the neckband and front facings to be best appreciated. By contrast, Japanese *kimono* are simple T-shaped garments with full sleeves, and the most intricate designs are usually across the back of the robe and around the lower edge; therefore, they are ideally suited to be hung high and flat against a blank wall by means of a pole running along the shoulder line and through the length of the sleeves. *Kimono* hung in this way are particularly effective in a tall, narrow space, such as a stairwell.

Chinese lacquer screens are avidly collected by Western Orientophiles for the exquisite quality of their colours and decoration. A four-panelled piece in gold and red on a black ground shows idealized landscapes with figures **(opposite above)**, while a slightly later coromandel screen has a central carved and painted design of a mandarin and his retinue, surrounded by a border of vases of flowers **(opposite below)**.

Oriental screens can be successfully used in Western homes for the dual purposes for which they were originally created; firstly, they fulfil a decorative role by portraying a scene in brilliant and resonant colours, and secondly they are useful room dividers, either making the interior more intimate or simply masking an area not considered worthy of public scrutiny. Mounted on a wall and displayed flat, an antique lacquered screen has a fascinating graphic appeal and one of its panels opens to give access to a bathroom **(left above)**, while a folded four-panel painted screen breaks up an awkward corner **(left below)**. In a Western building whose aesthetic is rigorously functional, the architect has taken up the lesson of space management from the Japanese in the provision of two suspended screens to give a sense of intimacy to a seating area **(opposite)**.

The subject matter of traditional Oriental screens reflects the ideals, aspirations and values of the societies responsible for their creation; hence, natural forms such as plants and flowers and real or imaginary beasts have a symbolic significance far beyond their considerable decorative qualities **(opposite above).** Our ancestors were also fascinated by the absence of Western-style depictions of perspectival space, as portrayed in the almost axionometric cityscape on an antique eight-panelled screen **(opposite below)**. However, perhaps the most appealing facet of Chinese screens is their astonishing craftsmanship and skilful rendering of detail, such as in the two eighteenth-century carved jade table screens **(above)**.

Decorative objects from the East suitable for use in Western interiors vary from fine and rare antiques to more financially accessible objects, which may also have a strictly practical use. This selection of jars, statuary and furniture **(left and left below)** is mainly from Thailand and typifies the range of Oriental artefacts readily available at specialist shops in the West; such screens, tables and mirrors bring a decorative and exotic air to any interior. Both Oriental object and technique are present in this corner of a splendid London living room **(opposite)**; a pair of rare seventeenth-century Chinese ceramic birds adorn the top of an eighteenth-century English lacquer commode.

Ornate mirrors from the Far East make a pleasing addition to Orientalist settings. The user of the lavishly carved Burmese dressing table **(above left)** kneels on the floor to apply cosmetics; the style of this piece reveals a profound Indian influence. A large mirror in an entrance hall adds to the illusion of space **(above right)**, while the form and workmanship of an elegant Indonesian dressing table and stool in a Balinese house is a fusion of native and colonial styles **(opposite)**.

The basic carcases of many Oriental storage cabinets and chests tend to be rectangular and rather solid in form, but they often carry extremely inventive detailing and workmanship. The rich, honey-coloured *huang huali* wood of a Chinese cabinet in two sections **(above)** has been intricately carved in light-relief to depict a continuous pattern of dragons chasing pearls, while a pair of cabinets in the same material **(centre)** have open fretwork panels in a geometric design. Smaller lacquered Japanese chests feature asymmetrical designs based on natural forms **(opposite above and below)**.

The Oriental options in bedding are many; the epitome of unobtrusive simplicity and comfort is undoubtedly the Japanese *futon*, or soft cotton mattress **(far left above)**, which can be folded to make seating or stored when not required **(left above)**. Enterprising Western manufacturers are currently reworking the traditional *futon*; a rectilinear 'four-poster' *futon*, hung with swathes of draped fabric, has an understated elegance **(left below)**.

By contrast, the traditional beds of Thailand have a rather more sensuous appeal because of their carved, curvilinear forms. In an uncluttered domestic setting in Spain **(left)**, an antique Thai bedbase harmonizes with a Burmese monastery chest, while the exuberant pierced carving of a high-sided bedframe in a Bangkok emporium **(below)** evokes a rather more opulent mood.

Contemporary Philippine manufacturers produce new furniture to traditional designs; a sense of intimacy in a large room **(opposite)** is achieved by the grouping of woven cane seats around a limed teak table.

The more rugged forms of Chinese bamboo and split cane furniture are extremely sturdy and have a pleasingly tactile appearance; they are especially effective visually when placed alongside a wide variety of other Oriental pieces, such as large Chinese baskets **(left)** or a collection of Tibetan religious artefacts **(below)**.

An entirely personal Oriental style can be created by combining the objects and artefacts of a number of countries in a single interior, purely out of a sense of pleasure in the final result. These three living rooms are in London **(above left)**, Belgium **(below left)** and Spain **(opposite)**, but they share a common understanding of the Oriental appreciation of adding visually appealing elements to everyday life.

The majority of Oriental furniture to be found in the West consists of simple, generally unadorned pieces, the materials of which are untreated beyond the use of coloured stains and varnish. However, smaller pieces are frequently intricately decorated, especially in the case of screens and ornamental small chests or boxes. The stunning craftsmanship of these antique Japanese pieces **(right)** reveals a remarkable facility with lacquer and inlay; the choice of subject matter reveals the fundamental Far Eastern preoccupations with nature and trade.

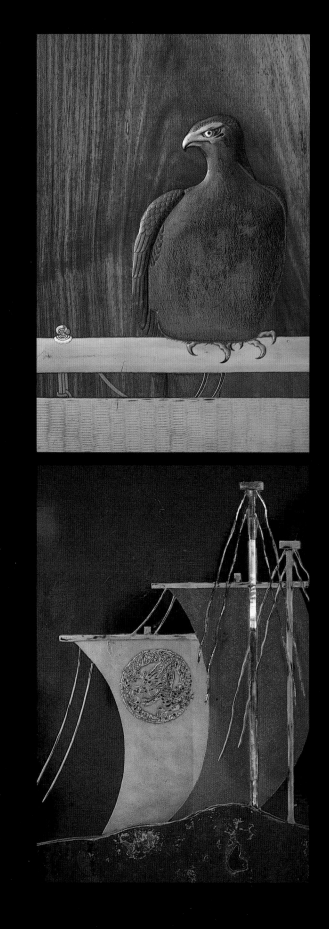

An elegantly simple Chinese rosewood cabinet with heavy brass fittings, from the last century.

Old Oriental garments are rapidly becoming collectors' items in the West, although they are still obtainable outside auction rooms and specialist dealers. Where space and finance do not allow the enthusiast to buy a complete garment, it is possible to come across parts of traditional Far Eastern dress, such as embroidered sleeve bands for Chinese robes, or portions of the highly ornate *obi* used to secure *kimono* around the upper torso; the delicately graduated colours and astonishing intricacy of needlework in these pieces make them ideal to be framed and displayed in smaller spaces. It is important that such antique textiles are hung out of direct daylight, as the dyes originally used were of vegetable origin, and they may gradually fade if constantly exposed to strong sunlight.

Having considered the alternatives available in the West for those seeking to use Oriental furniture and furnishings in their own home, it is important to briefly assess the sources available for buying old or new pieces. Naturally, the older and more exquisite the item, the more likely it is to be the preserve of wealthy connoisseurs and collectors, and most major Western cities have a flourishing community of specialist dealers who can meet the requirements of their patrons through an informal network of contacts, which often stretches across several countries. However, for the top end of the Oriental antiques trade, it is vital that objects are in very good condition – those items which have been damaged, warped or cracked are less desirable to serious collectors, although they are often still extremely attractive, and when these appear at auctions their price is more variable.

House auctions and second-hand emporia often prove fruitful locations for discovering authentic Eastern or Oriental-style furniture. Considering the 'unfurnished' look of many traditional Oriental interiors, it is perhaps surprising to consider the vast variety of antique and second-hand furniture to be found in Western house sales, junk shops and public auctions. During the last century, the vogue for Chinese and Japanese goods created a massive market for small, lightweight pieces of furniture, and Far Eastern craftsmen and merchants were quick to respond to the demand, often working from designs provided by British or American traders and entrepreneurs. Throughout the 1880s, no self-respecting household was complete without a liberal quota of bamboo tables and chairs, bookcases and 'whatnots', many of which originated in Shanghai, but could be easily bought or ordered from the most traditional and high-class department stores. At one point, demand so outstripped supply that Western furniture designers and cabinet-makers began to produce pieces which mimicked the appearance of lacquer by a process known a 'japanning', applying an ingenious combination of paint and varnish.

It is well worth considering the thriving market in reproduction furniture; traditional designs continue to be exported from Thailand, Hong Kong and China, and can be purchased in many department stores and Oriental emporia throughout the West. Lacquered cabinets from southern China and folding screens from Beijing are often reasonably priced and extremely decorative, while simple dining sets and altar tables in carved satinwood or blackwood greatly enhance the Oriental ambience in Western dwellings.

Care should be taken in the handling of lacquered and wooden furniture from the Far East, whether antique or contemporary. The extremes of temperature and dry atmospheres found in many Western centrally-heated homes can adversely affect the frames and finishes of furniture. It is therefore important that Oriental furniture is placed away from direct heat sources, such as radiators, and if possible the atmosphere should be made more humid by using strategically-placed reservoirs of moisture, such as well-watered plants. A useful tactic is to place saucers of water under tables out of public view.

Where furniture cannot be easily obtained or accommodated within an already crowded room, the would-be Orientalist can nevertheless achieve an impressive effect by taking advantage of Far Eastern furnishings, textiles and wall hangings. With a little forethought, careful planning and judicious selection, an Eastern ambience can be created in the most uncompromising Western interior.

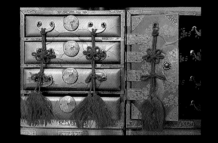

DECORATIVE DETAIL

Attention to detail is an integral feature of every aspect of Oriental life, from the wrapping of presents to the attractive presentation of food. In the case of Far Eastern architecture, art and design, the correct and appropriate use of decorative detail is considered to be paramount, as is apparent from the examples already shown. In order to create a convincing Oriental-style interior in a Western setting, care should be taken in initially identifying typically Far Eastern details, colour schemes, materials and objects, and then using them with confidence, displaying them to their best advantage, and adding life and vitality to any setting. In a small London apartment **(opposite)**, the unifying colour scheme is derived from a colour range traditionally associated with China; Chinese folding chairs bring an interesting sculptural liveliness to the room, and a fascinating collection of south-east Asian statuary holds the eye.

To many in the West, the idea of creating their own 'Oriental' interior is highly appealing, but is often tempered by practical considerations, such as the restrictions of space and finance. However, with a little imagination and application, an Oriental effect can be achieved in even the most prosaically Western home. By assessing the potential of any interior, and then consciously acquiring and applying appropriate objects, materials, textures, colours and motifs, it is possible to create an imaginative, inspired and highly personal Orientalist setting.

Attention to visual, sensual and cultural detail is an essential characteristic of Oriental life, permeating not only the somewhat rarified atmosphere of temples, palaces and plush restaurants, but also dictating the selection of dishes for the simplest meal, the display of vegetables and herbal medicines on market stalls, the wrapping of simple gifts or the sweeping brushstrokes of a handwritten signboard.

Everyday objects are made with care and respect for their materials; tools and domestic artefacts are cared for and valued, not only because of their traditional scarcity, but because of their inherent 'spirit', which should be respected. Similarly, little distinction is made between 'beautiful' objects and 'functional' ones, because any object which is skilfully crafted and well-designed is automatically felt to be pleasing to the eye. Nevertheless, anything which is superfluous to immediate requirements within the household is stored until needed, resulting in the elimination of the insignificant and the consequent liberation of space, so that those features which are deemed satisfying or enriching are displayed to their best advantage and to the aesthetic benefit of the observer.

The significance of colour is an important factor in determining the look of much of the Far East, as colour is used not only for its decorative or mood-changing qualities, but also for its symbolic significance. The ancient Chinese believed that the 'five colours' of blue, red, yellow, white and black corresponded to the 'five elements' of wood, fire, earth, metal and water. Consequently, the ideal balance of colours combined these hues; however, in time, all colours were believed to impart certain qualities, and even today particular colours are deliberately chosen for their individual connotations throughout those countries influenced by Chinese culture. Red is considered to be generally auspicious, and therefore it is the preferred colour for bridal costumes in China, Korea and Japan, to avert the negative forces of *feng shui* in Hong Kong and Taiwan, and for the envelopes containing gifts of money given throughout the region at New Year. White is the traditional colour of purity and so it is used for mourning dress in many countries, while green symbolizes rebirth and longevity. Yellow was the colour traditionally only worn in the Imperial Court of the Chinese Emperor, and therefore is associated with authority in all its forms, while blue symbolizes peace, eternity and blessings from Heaven.

For interiors, the ideal Oriental colour scheme is an overwhelming emphasis upon the neutral, coupled with 'highlights' of those colours deemed most appropriate to the function of a room. For example, the dominant tones of *yang* colours (red, yellow, purple or grey) are best used in a room where important decisions have to be made and positive action taken, while *yin* colours (green, blue and white) are better suited to rooms for contemplation, consideration and study. Similarly, the motifs and designs used to decorate the home are selected according to the qualities they are believed to embody. The sense of cultural affiliation with the forces of Nature is evident in the continuing aesthetic preoccupation with landscapes and natural forms, depicted in views of stylized mountains and idealized cloud and wave formations, but the forms of more prosaic birds and beasts are also believed to imbue the inhabitants with certain highly desirable characteristics; thus tortoises symbolize longevity, while bats (in stark contrast to their Western connotations) are the bringers of happiness and light-heartedness. The monogamous relationship of ducks is believed to bode well for newly-married couples, while carp are symbols of vitality and fertility: 'Boys' Day' in Japan is still marked by the flying of paper carp pennants from the roof of those family homes with sons.

The symbolism of particular flora is of major concern to Oriental families, so that orchids are traditionally the flower of welcome in Thailand, while a graphic combination of cracked ice and prunus blossom in China is traditionally used to signify a major age difference in a newly married couple, or a second marriage after widowhood, or on a more general level, the coming of spring and a sense of renewed vitality.

As so much of traditional Oriental life was dependent upon the cycle of the seasons and concomitant success of the harvest of the staple food crop, it is hardly surprising that the passing of the seasons is still marked with festivals and rituals appropriate to the time of year. Therefore, the adaptability of the traditional Oriental interior was constantly put to the test, and one major feature of the attention paid to decorative detail in the Far East was the constantly changing cycle of the objects used to decorate the setting. Therefore, the mood created by a room was felt to be in harmony with the seasons or important events affecting family life, and the changes to the interior were created through meticulous attention to detail.

Many of the items used to enhance the traditional or modern Oriental interior have long been available in the West; indeed, their aesthetic qualities made them popular imports. The earliest artefacts from the Orient to be avidly sought in the West were ceramics shipped from China; even the English word 'china', meaning porcelain, is believed to be derived from the name of the ruling Chin Dynasty. Undoubtedly some of the most beautiful porcelain, celadon and stoneware in the world was developed and produced in the 'Middle Kingdom'. Despite strenuous attempts to safeguard the secrets of Chinese glazing and firing techniques, the recipes for ceramics technology gradually spread throughout the adjacent countries and were much imitated by European manufacturers, although the vast quantities of exports to the West bears witness to the continuing appeal of Chinese colours, finishes and motifs. Within

The *cho-fa* or decorative roof finial of Thailand is used as a protective device on temple roofs and is laden with symbolic significance; its distinctive sinuous form is intended to guard against evil spirits and mishaps. Great store is placed on using precious materials for *cho-fa* and they are frequently covered with gold leaf or inlaid with precious stones **(opposite)**. These abstract sculptural forms evolved from the belief in the protective powers of the *naga* or mythical water serpent of Thailand **(opposite right above and below, above and above right)**; when they have outlived their usefulness, the *cho-fa* may make a fascinating sculptural addition to an Oriental-style interior **(right below)**.

the past few years the availability of antique Chinese ceramics has dwindled rapidly, as the Chinese Government has recently prohibited the mass exportation of its older cultural artefacts.

It is still possible, indeed likely, that concerted foraging in secondhand shops and open air markets will reveal antique Chinese ceramics, given the volume of old pieces which are still in circulation in Europe and America. Slightly damaged pieces do not usually command the attention of serious collectors, yet they are highly appealing and very decorative. Similarly, the rather more rugged and utilitarian ceramics of China can be extremely attractive; of particular appeal are the large scale 'Double Happiness' stoneware pots of the late nineteenth century. The character for 'happiness' (pronounced 'shi') was duplicated in blue on a white background, and these jars would be filled with foodstuffs and given to rural Chinese newly-weds to celebrate their marriage in the hope that they would bring each other contentment. These vessels were the basic food containers of every Chinese kitchen in the last century, and consequently they are not greatly regarded in their own country, but in an Oriental-style setting they can be highly pleasing.

In the time-honoured tradition of reworking the themes of the past, modern manufacturers throughout the Far East are also producing a wide variety of ceramics using the materials and designs of the past. Shanghai factories are currently experimenting with crackle-glaze celadon ware with great success, while companies in Hong Kong employ large workforces to hand-paint bodies made in Macao in the traditional colours and patterns of 'famille rose' and 'famille verte'. The perennial favourite remains 'blue and white', the underglaze cobalt blue historically associated with China, although contemporary manufacturers now include Thailand, Macao and the Philippines, all of which are becoming increasingly successful in producing economical and attractive decorative pieces and flatware.

Mass-produced Japanese ceramics are also available in most large cities and, although more expensive than the products of their Asian neighbours, tend to be slightly more subtle and 'earthy' in appearance and coloration. Interestingly, Japanese manufacturers frequently go to great lengths to imitate the appearance of hand-crafting, particularly in those ceramics where the design appears to be hand-painted. Sparingly used, these items can be highly attractive and very impressive.

The rôle to be played by Far Eastern textiles in creating an Oriental style interior has already been discussed, but it cannot be overstressed that individual old pieces or modern replicas can be decisive in achieving a successful effect. During the last century, heavily embroidered wool or silk Chinese shawls were highly fashionable in Europe and America; they were deliberately produced to suit what were perceived as Western tastes, yet in materials, motifs and workmanship, they remain thoroughly Eastern. Although often slightly damaged or worn, Chinese shawls and wraps still appear at auctions and in junk shops. Their riotous colours and lustrous sheen are best displayed draped across the back of a settee, thrown across a bed or displayed on a wall.

Burmese and Thai *kalagas* similarly make excellent wall-hangings because of their bejewelled, ornate opulence and rich colours; they frequently feature scenes from the life of the Buddha or local mythology. The materials used in them are often deliberately aged by leaving the background fabric, rhinestones and sequins exposed to the extremes of weather before making up the pieces into a highly decorative design. Bordered by bands of Thai silk and hung against an otherwise blank wall, the exuberance of the pattern and richness of effect can make a highly dramatic display.

For decorative and highly distinctive textile pieces to hang on walls, a vast choice is available. In America, West Coast dealers occasionally have *nobori* in stock; these are the traditional tall, narrow cotton banners of Japan, often as much as four metres in length. The fabric is cotton, but the designs are hand-painted scenes from Japanese legend or history. As the surface was treated with vegetable dyes, the once-brilliant colours have often faded to softer hues of indigo blue, dark rose and gold, although the motifs and figures remain vibrant and compelling. *Nobori* are shown to their best advantage hung vertically in a tall, empty wall space, or laterally across a ceiling. Similarly, in a high-roofed interior, a collection of assorted traditional paper and cloth kites from a variety of Far Eastern sources would greatly enhance the space if suspended on almost invisible filaments from the ceiling. As these items are customarily associated with festivities and celebrations, their forms and colours are frequently vibrant and arresting.

A similar effect can be achieved on walls, by combining a number of related items from diverse sources. Native musical instruments often have beautiful and impressive sculptural shapes; traditional dance and drama are an integral part of the Oriental lifestyle, so that the masks found throughout the region have a significance both decorative and cultural. The pâpier-maché opera masks of Beijing are among the best known examples; the faces portray characters both real and divine from Chinese cultural history, and are more or less human in scale. By contrast, the mythical creatures portrayed in mask form in Balinese cultures, such as the *barang* or lion's head, are large in size and somewhat intimidating in appearance, but they make a superb display, adding colour and vitality to any interior.

Rather more subtle examples of Oriental craftsmanship can be combined in an equally successful way; the folding fans of China, Japan, Korea and Singapore form wonderfully graphic shapes on a plain surface and recall the patterns of textile designs. Tiny, exquisite artefacts originally intended to ornament the body, such as Chinese fine combs and Japanese hairpins are displayed to their best effect against a dark background which brings out the richness of their materials.

The principle of displaying numerous small-scale decorative objects together is one which occurs throughout the Orient, and it can be used to great effect in Western settings.

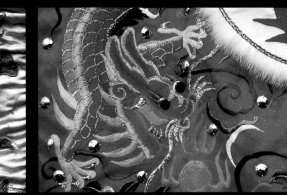

Interesting combinations of colour and motif are not necessarily confined to the finest of Oriental textiles. The traditional Thai silk embroidery **(left)** is clearly of high and enduring quality, but this display in a London emporium of decorative cushions **(opposite)** from all over the Far East shows a source of decorative delight at very modest cost.

Miniaturization is a typical characteristic of much of traditional and modern Oriental design, so that tiny objects are often extremely intricate in their form and decoration. The epitome of this approach is perhaps the Japanese *netsuke* or carved belt toggle, which was used to secure pouches and small carrying cases through the *obi*, or sash, of the *kimono*-clad wearer. The naturalistic forms of these tiny, exquisite sculptures make them highly sought after by collectors, but a number of Western museums now sell good-quality reproductions in a variety of modern materials which capture the essence of these tiny but vital forms.

To the purist or connoisseur, the idea of reproduction is anathema – yet, ironically, much of the currency in modern Oriental design is based on reworking the past. For the would-be Orientalist on a limited budget, the opportunities to acquire entirely traditional styles of Oriental art and artefacts has never been equalled, particularly in the field of graphics.

Perhaps the best-known of the graphic arts of the Far East are Japanese woodblock prints; they were bought by Japanese travellers in the same way that we might buy postcards, perhaps for their depiction of regional beauty spots, the strength of a local *sumo* wrestler or performance of a famous actor. *Kimono* merchants used them as sales aids, because they often featured the latest sartorial trends of the tastemakers of the day, the fashionable courtesans, who inhabited the larger cities' pleasure quarters. Although now avidly collected in both their country of origin and in the West, Japanese woodblock prints were originally regarded as mere printed ephemera, but both in their original form and in the high-quality reproductions widely available, they embody the aesthetics of much of Oriental style.

Hanging scrolls are the epitome of Oriental art forms, and while original paintings are frequently extremely costly, a factory in Beijing continues to produce modern, handpainted copies of traditional paintings ready mounted upon fabric backing for the export market; the format and subtle appeal of these graphics are highly suitable for use in tall spaces such as stairwells.

The subject of calligraphy is one which bears some analysis; the Chinese 'conceptual' approach to the graphic depiction of language was originally derived from the use of hieroglyphics, and subsequently spread throughout much of the Far East. Part of the initial appeal of travelling in the countries of the Orient is doubtlessly derived from the strangeness of the language, particularly to Westerners accustomed to a mere twenty-six 'building blocks' with which to depict the infinitely subtle nuances of communication. Furthermore, a theoretical combination of over 50,000 characters provides a fertile source of symbolic associations with 'fortuitous' or 'malignant' forms in everyday life.

While the mastery of calligraphy is widely considered in the Far East to be the high point of human achievement, it should not be forgotten that the forces and forms of nature are also given due respect in the Oriental setting, because of their similar ability to evoke the essence of man's existence. Natural forms are believed to concentrate the mind and stimulate the consciousness through meditation, and thus the unique formation of weather-beaten 'scholars' rocks' are revered as objects of contemplation, particularly in those countries where the ancient culture of China has had a profound influence. Similarly the deliberate cultivation of 'nature in miniature' through the medium of *bonsai* or miniature landscapes, is regarded as a worthy art form because it provokes both an identification with the eternal cycle of growth and decay combined with an appreciation of the interaction between man and his environment.

The essence of the Oriental approach to the creation of a successful interior relies upon the elimination of mindless clutter, and the enhancement of those objects and artefacts which stimulate the inhabitants and appeal to their senses. Whether the style adopted to achieve this effect is purist or eclectic is a matter of personal choice; for example, a small, dark room would benefit greatly from redecoration inspired by the traditional Japanese approach: plain, light-coloured walls, monochromatic flooring and built-in storage would simplify and clarify the interior, making it a suitable setting for a collection of simple but aesthetically appealing objects, such as *bonsai* trees or a selection of Oriental ceramics. The atmosphere in such a room would be calm and restful; this might be a suitable scheme for a workroom or study.

By contrast, an air of exotic opulence can be achieved through combining a variety of Far Eastern textiles and textures, particularly if the colour range is drawn from those hues typically associated with the Orient, such as cinnabar red, black and gold, Chinese yellow or jade green. Similarly, objects bearing popular traditional motifs, such as sinuous dragons, flying cranes, prunus blossom or stylized wave and cloud formations can reinforce the sense of eclectic Orientalism.

A selection of bamboo wedding baskets and details from mainland China **(opposite)**. Traditionally, young couples would receive wedding presents in these containers. The three tiers separate, providing a compact and portable method of storing numerous household items. They make striking free-standing ornaments, either placed on the floor or on a large article of furniture, such as a chest.

The careful selection of a few Oriental artefacts adds visual impact and drama to a Western interior **(right)**. An antique Japanese *tansu*, a painted Chinese wedding basket and a colourful Tibetan mask of papier-mâché provide vivid contrasts to the cool, rectilinear simplicity of this hallway.

The startling variety of shapes and forms to be found in traditional Thai and Burmese lacquer bowls and food stands is a manifestation of the Oriental desire to act appropriately on particular occasions. Families consider it important to show respect and hospitality to their visitors by serving food in the correct and most attractive container **(opposite)**. The resonant colour of an antique Burmese lacquer food bowl glows from its monochromatic setting, and its simple form sits perfectly on an overtly Modernist table by Eileen Gray **(left)**.

The use of ornate Japanese lacquerware in an otherwise minimalist Western setting introduces resonant, vibrant colour and fascinating detail. The fan-shaped stacking box, nesting trays and armrest are shown to their best advantage combined on a low table in the drawing room **(right)**.

The low-level viewpoint and the uncluttered simplicity of the hallway **(opposite)** is heightened by the careful positioning of three exquisitely lacquered retinue trunks below framed *ukiyo-e* woodblock prints, while the solid carcase of the chest provides a perfect plinth for the bizarre forms of a *bonsai* miniature tree.

Collecting and displaying Oriental objects together can be visually satisfying and add to the character of a room. The smooth, rounded forms and the rich colours of a variety of red and black lacquer bowls from Thailand and Burma are shown to their best advantage housed in alcove shelving around a Spanish fireplace **(left)**.

A Japanese *kaidan-dansu* or staircase chest (above left) provides a fascinating stepped display case for pieces of Indonesian ivory and Ban Prasat Thai pots. Antique blue and white Chinese porcelain sits well on contemporary shelving **(above right)**.

Old Oriental pieces surprise and intrigue
the viewer when placed in a contemporary Western
setting. A wooden figure of the Buddha sits serenely
in a stairwell **(above)**, while a Japanese *hibachi*, or
brazier, provides a home for houseplants
(opposite).

Predominantly monochromatic settings allow the colours and textures of Oriental pieces to become fascinating focal points. A collection of Japanese lacquered miniature furniture sits jewel-like on a glass table **(above left)**; the rugged simplicity of two Tibetan trunks adds weight and solidity to a hallway **(above right)**, while a Spanish open-plan drawing room houses modern Philippino cane furniture and an angle of the stairs houses a woven basket from the Karen hill-tribes of Thailand **(opposite)**.

Oriental statuary has a particularly evocative power and can be used to create or define the atmosphere of a room. An uplit Khmer mask **(left)** has a surreal, disembodied quality, while the antique stone Buddha simply placed as a central piece in a living room provides an atmosphere of calm and tranquility **(opposite)**.

A French apartment which uses Oriental figures and artefacts as focal points; hanging bamboo blinds cover the windows and divide the drawing room, while allowing light to filter through; an altar table supports a pair of red Chinese vases and a seventeenth-century *cloisonné* bowl from the Imperial Palace **(left above)**. Large scale sculptural pieces dominate this interior, including a rare antique Buddhist statue, carved wooden buffalo from Indonesia **(left below)** and a mounted *cho-fa* or Thai temple roof finial **(opposite)**.

The intricacy of form and the delicacy of decorative detail of eighteenth-century chinoiserie is recalled in a Western setting; ceramic Chinese *fo* dogs guard the bedchamber **(left)**, Indonesian animals settle on a table **(below)** while a precocity of carving of stylized clouds decorates a Chinese table **(opposite)**, below which is the reclining figure of an eighteenth-century Burmese Buddha.

The materials and shapes of Oriental boxes and votive food containers have a particular aesthetic charm and make excellent additions to Western settings: a selection of Burmese lacquered religious ceremonial food boxes **(above left and right below)** and a Philippino wood box **(right above)**. Thai inlaid lacquer boxes make a decorative addition to a dressing table **(opposite)**.

Rugs and textiles are among the most easily transportable and durable of all decorative artefacts from the Far East. Their stylized motifs and vibrant colours add an authentic Oriental atmosphere to Western interiors, as in this London house **(below)**. This room is dominated by a tiger rug from Tibet; these are especially popular in the West for their rich imagery and traditional associations. Indonesian rugs make an important contribution to the sense of luxury and exuberance in this London apartment **(opposite)**.

Combinations of small utensils and artefacts can look very effective when combined in a restricted space; the skilled workmanship, quality of materials and miniature size of many Oriental decorative forms makes them ideal for display in Western homes. A collection of various Thai black lacquered boxes **(left above)**, Japanese lacquered haircombs **(left below)**, Tibetan purses **(opposite left)** or assorted Oriental ceramics **(opposite below right)** makes a delicate display – an effect suggestive of the careful arrangement of traditional tea ceremony utensils in a Japanese setting **(opposite above right)**. Care and respect for even small and apparently insignificant objects inform much of Oriental design and decoration.

Decorative details can also play a vital part in creating an Oriental-style garden; Thai craftsmen are extremely adept at creating reproduction 'antique' statues, such as a mythical Khmer figure **(above left)**, while the *fo* dog or guardian lion is becoming increasingly available in the West, as modern Chinese marble statues in traditional forms are currently manufactured in Tianjin and are available in many major Western cities **(above centre)**. Ceramic vessels and wooden mill cogs provoke curiosity, especially when partially concealed by verdant undergrowth **(above right and opposite)**.

Picture credits

All the photographs in this book are the work of Michael Freeman, except the following;
p.4 Thames & Hudson; p.5 Futon Company (top left), Japan National Tourist Organisation (centre left), Agence Top (photo. Pascal Hinous) (centre right); pp.6, 7 Peter Cook; p.9 Michael Jenner (a.), Sotheby's (b.); pp.10, 11 Thames & Hudson; p.12 Sotheby's; p.13 Fine Art Photographic Library (a.l. and b.), Siân Evans (a.r); p.14 Thames & Hudson; p.15 Siân Evans (a.), British Architecture Library/R.I.B.A (centre), Thames & Hudson (b.); p.16 Luca Invernezzi (a.); p.17 Luca Invernezzi; p.22 Luca Invernezzi (a.); p.23 Japan National Tourist Organisation (a.); p.35 Hong Kong Tourism Authority (b.1); p.36 Luca Invernezzi; p.41 Luca Invernezzi (b.r.); p.47 Bill Tingey (r.); p.48 Luca Invernezzi (a.), Bill Tingey; (b.), Siân Evans (second from top); p.50 Fine Art Photographic Library; pp.70, 71, 72, 73, 74, 75, 79 Bill Tingey; p.80 Hong Kong Tourism Authority (a.), Bill Tingey (second from top), Futon Co. (b.); p.81 Agence Top (photo Pascal Hinous); pp.106, 107 Blueprint; pp.110, 111, 112, 113, 114, 115 Keyphotos (photo Kikutani); p.118 Agence Top (photo Pascal Hinous); p.119 Photobright; p.124 Agence Top (photo Pascal Hinous); pp.130, 131 Peter Cook; pp.132, 133 Keyphotos (photo Kikutani); p.135 Peter Cook; p.136 Hong Kong Tourism Authority (second from top), Mimi Lipton (b.); p.139 Bridgeman Art Library; p.142 Sotheby's; p.146 Sotheby's; p.150 Sotheby's (a. and b.l.), Sheila Fitzjones (r.); p.159 Sotheby's; p.160 Edimedia (photo R. Guillemot) (a.), Edimedia (photo J. Guillot) (b.); pp.162, 163 Bridgeman Art Library; p.164 Sheila Fitzjones; p.165 Michael Boys; p.168 Sotheby's; p.169 Bridgeman Art Library (a.r. and b.r.); p.170 Futon Co.; p.174 Agence Top (photo Pascal Hinous) (b.); p.178 Sotheby's; p.180 Agence Top (photo Pascal Hinous) (second from top); pp.204, 205 Agence Top (photo Pascal Hinouis); p.206 Edimedia (photo R. Guillemot); p.207 Edimedia (photo R. Guillemot); pp.208, 209 Edimedia (photo R. Guillemot). All photographs on the jacket are by Michael Freeman.
The photograph on p.8 © Her Majesty Queen Elizabeth II is reproduced by gracious permission of Her Majesty Queen Elizabeth II (photo Michael Feeeman).

Acknowledgments

The authors and publishers wish to extend especial thanks to the people and organizations listed below for their substantial help and guidance in the creation of this book.

Percy Barkes and Delia Su, Charlotte Barnes, Beagle Gallery, Jean-Michel Beurdeley, Michael Birch, Yui Ying Brown, The Buddhist Centre, Carroll, Dempsey & Thirkell, Odile Cavendish, Margaret Caselton, David Chipperfield Associates, Peter Cook, Shirley Day, Michael Dean, Walter Donahue, Kevin Donnelly, Françoise Durand of Agence Top, Fine Art Photographs, Sheila Fitzjones, Gerda Flockinger, Jonathan Gale, Caroline Gearey of the Bridgeman Art Library, Felicity Golden, Stephen Greenberg and Dean Hawkes, Khum Fa Ham, Lillian Hochhauser, Hong Kong Tourism Authority, Takashi Inaba, Japan National Tourist Organisation, Lena and Talal Kanafani, Korean National Tourist Corporation, The Lacquer Factory, Saigon, C. T. Loo et Cie, Hansjorg Mayer, Hidetoshi Mujagi, Klaus Müller, Sylvia Napier, Neal Street East, Ambassadress Josephine de Oliveira Maia, Old Chiangmai Cultural Centre, Rama Antiques, Ruth Orbach, Tjokorda Patra, Miranda Rothschild, The Saigon Tourist Office, David Salmon, The Siam Society of Bangkok, Paul Sibbering, Mark Slattery, Charlie Smith of Remote Treasures, Sotheby's Chinese Department, Geneviève de Taragon of Edimedia, Jim Thomson, Bill Tingey, Anongnart Ulapathorn, The Urasenke Foundation, Steve Vidler, Dieter and Susie von Boehm-Bering, Daniel and Thomas White, Henry Woods-Wilson. The apartment illustrated on p. 81 was designed by Daigre et Rybar.

Select Bibliography

Conner, Patrick, *Oriental Architecture in the West*, London, 1979

Dinkel, John, *The Royal Pavilion, Brighton*, London, 1983

Engel, Heino, *Measure and Construction of the Japanese House*, Vermont and Tokyo, 1985

Hibi, Sadao, *Japanese Detail* (3 vols.), San Francisco and London, 1989

Inoue, Mitsuo, *Space in Japanese Architecture*, Tokyo and New York, 1985

Invernezzi, Luca and William Warren, *Living in Thailand*, London, 1988

Japan Art and Culture Association, *Charles Rennie Mackintosh*, Tokyo, 1985

Kaufmann, Edgar and Ben Raeburn, *Frank Lloyd Wright: Writings and Buildings*, New York, 1960

Kim, H. Edward, *The Korean Smile*, Seoul, 1983

Lee, Sherman , E., *A History of Far Eastern Art*, London, 1975

Lee, Sherman E., *Japanese Decorative Style*, New York, 1972

Lip, Dr. Evelyn, *Feng Shui for the Home*, New York, 1985

Powell, Andrew, *Living Buddhism*, London, 1989

Slesin, Suzanne, Stafford Cliff and Daniel Rozensztroch, *Japanese Style*, New York and London, 1987

Wichmann, Siegfried, *Japonisme*, London, 1981

Wright, Susan M., *The Delcorative Arts in the Victorian Period*, London, 1989

Galleries and Suppliers

This directory contains a selective list of sources for Oriental furniture, objects and art. While every effort has been made to include as many diverse sources as possible, it should not be regarded as an exhaustive list. Similarly, while every attempt was made to ensure that all of the information given is correct, we cannot be held responsible for any inaccuracies which may unintentionally have occured.

Australia

Nomad Gallery, 262 Oxford Street, Paddington, NSW 2021   331 5015

Belgium

Luc Ritter, Rue Ernest Allard 17, 1000 Bruxelles, Belgium 512 46 79
Lucien Van de Velde, Schildedreef 1, 2230 Schilde, Belgium   383 63 94

France

Jean-Michel Beurdeley, 200 Bd. St-Germain, Paris (1) 45 48 97 86
Eileen Lesouëf, 2 Place du Palais Royal, 75001 Paris (1) 42 61 58 40

Hawaii

Robyn Buntin, 900A Maunakea Street, Honolulu, Hawaii 96817   (808) 523 5913

Hong Kong

Ancient Chinese Antiques, 199 Hollywood Road., G/F,. 541 0183
Ancient Features, No. 2B, G/F, The Centre Mark, 287–99 Queen's Road Central   541 9813
Arts of China, Shop 325, Hong Kong Hotel Arcade, Canton Road, Kowloon   730 5073
Cathay Arts Co, B3, 6/F, Friends' House, 6C Carnarvon Rd., T.S.T. Kowloon   739 1172
Jade House, 3040 Hong Kong Hotel Shopping Arcade, Kowloon   735 7491
Kosilk Co. Ltd, L1–6 New World Centre, Tsimshatsui, Kowloon   369 8644
Store, 142 Hollywood Road, G/F   540 4772
China Handicraft Co. Ltd, 21 Lock Road, 1st Floor, Box 95924, T.S.T Post Office, Kowloon   366 9406
C.L.MA Antiques, 24, Hollywood Road, Ground Floor, Central   525 4369
Teresa Coleman Fine Arts, 37 Wyndham St., Ground Floor, Central   545 9330/5675
Martin Fung, 1/Fl., Cat Street Galleries, 38 Lok Ku Road, Central   545 9330/5675
Hanart Gallery, 40 Hollywood Road   541 0941
Hanlin Gallery, 30 Hollywood Road   522 4479
Charlotte Horstmann & Gerald Godfrey Ltd, Ocean Terminal, Kowloon   735 7167
Kai-Yin & Co. Ltd, 2 Wellington Street   524 3108
Kander's, 56A–58 Hollywood Road, Central   544 2215
Fred Lee Gallery, 34 G/F Lyndhurst Terrace, Central   854 4636
Alvin Lo & Co. Ltd., 314 Exchange Square Two, Central 524 3395
Lai Loy & Son Antiques Ltd., 138 Hollywood Road   547 6145
Ming Gallery, Ground Floor, Parklane Building, 233 Queen's Road, Central   541 2031
The Nishiki Gallery, 304 The Podium, Tower One, Exchange Square, Central   845 2551
Plum Blossoms Gallery, 305–7 Exchange Square One   521 2189
Sovereign Company, Shop No. L1–80, New World Centre, 18–24 Salisbury Road, Tsimshatsui, Kowloon   369 5666
Tong-In Antique Gallery, G24, G/F., Hankow Centre, No. 5–15 Hankow Road, Tsimshatsui, Kowloon   369 1406

Wah Tung China Co., 12/F–17/F & 20/F./, Grand Marine Ind. Bldg, 3 Yue Fung St., Tin Wan Hill Rd., Aberdeen, Hong Kong   873 2272
Wing Hing Co., R128 Regent Shopping Arcade, 18 Salisbury Road, Kowloon   366 4923
Grace Wu Bruce Co. Ltd., (by appointment)   845 0840
Ying Chuan Tang Ltd, 29 Hollywood Road, Lower Ground Floor, Central   543 8466/8514

Japan

Daijindo Gallery Ltd, 6–7–5–107 Minami Aoyama, Minato-Ku, Tokyo 107   (09) 486 5091
Michael Dunn Ltd., 605 Mita Mansion, Mita 2–8–12, Minato-Ku, Tokyo 108   (03) 451 8735
Kurofune Antiques, 7–7–4– Roppongi, Minato-ku, Tokyo   (03) 479 1552
Ohno Oriental Art Galleries Co., No. 31–23, 2-chome, Yushima, Bunkyo-ku, Tokyo 113   (03) 811 4365
Shimojo Art Co. Ltd., Nichiei Bldg, 1F 4–8–3, Roppongi, Minato-Ku, Tokyo 106   (03) 401 8460/8470
Suichiko-Do, 7–108, Ginza, Chuo-Ku, Tokyo 104 (03) 572 0707

Singapore

Asiatic Fine Arts, 19 Tanglin Road, #03–54 Tanglin Shopping Centre, Singapore 1024   (65) 736 0957
Bareo Gallery, 19 Tanglin Road, #02–02/41, Tanglin Shopping Centre, Singapore 1024   (65) 737 3211
Kwok Gallery, 545 Orchard Road #03–01, Far East Shopping Centre, Singapore 0923   (65) 235 2516

Switzerland

Charles Rochat & Cie, 9 rue Rousseau, CH 1201, Geneva   (4122) 738 26 25

Taiwan

Bai Win, No 5 Lane 10, Chung Cheng Rd., Sec. 2, Taipei (02) 871 4943
Hanart Gallery, 104 Chung Shan North Road Sec 5, Taipei   (02) 882 9772
Kander's, 4 & 5 Fl., 230 Sec. 4, Chung Shiao E. Rd., Taipei   (02) 776 5858
Newworkshop, 1–8, Hou Chou Tzu, Hsien Hsiao Li, Tamsui   (02) 623 8052/3/4
C.C. Teng & Co., 3F–2 No. 6, Sec. 1, Shin Sheng S. Rd., Taipei   (02) 394 9019

Thailand

Elephant House, 67/12 Soi Phra Phinit, Soi Suan Phlu, Sathorn Tai Road, Bangkok 10120   286 5280
Lotus, Parichart Court, The Bangkok Regent, 155–7 Rajdamri Road, Bangkok 10500
Rama Antiques, 2nd Floor Oriental Plaza, 30–1 Chartered Bank Lane, Bangkok 10500, Thailand   235 7991, 235 9907

United Kingdom

Beagle Gallery, 303 Westbourne Grove, London W11   (071) 229 9524
John R. Berwald, Stand H10/11, Grays in the Mews, 1/7 Davis Mews, London W1Y 1AR   (071) 629 3191
Bluett & Sons Ltd., 48 Davies Street, London W1Y 1LD (071) 629 4018/3397
Brandt Oriental Antiques, 771 Fulham Road, London SW6   (071) 731 6835
Odile Cavendish, (by appointment only), 14 Lowndes Street, London SW1   (071) 243 1668
The Chinese Collection, 1 Goodwins Court, London WC2 (071) 836 1342
The Conran Shop, Michelin House, 81 Fulham Road, London SW3   (071) 589 7401
Futon Co., Ltd., 138 Notting Hill Gate, London W11   (071) 727 9252
Marilyn Garrow, Antique Textiles, 6 The Broadway, London SW13   (081) 392 1655

A substantial collection of Chinese blue and white ceramics.

Gerald Godfrey Far Eastern Art, 104 Mount Street, London W1   (071) 409 2777
Katie Jones, No. 126, Grays Antique Market, 58 Davies Street, London W1   (071) 493 1261
Kelly Hoppen & Charlotte Barnes Interiors, 32 Roland Gardens, London SW7   (071) 373 6197
Robert Kleiner & Co. Ltd., 11 Primrose Mansions, Prince of Wales Drive, London SW11 4ED   (071) 622 5462
The Oriental Department, Liberty PLC, Regent Street, London W1   (071) 734 1234
Loon Fung Importers Ltd, 118 Shaftesbury Avenue, London W1   (071) 437 3353
S Marchant & Son, 120 Kensington Church Street, London W8 4BH   (071) 229 5319
Adrian Maynard, 91c Jermyn Street, London SW1   (071) 930 08008
Mitsukiku, The Japanese Shop, 15 Old Brompton Road, London SW7   (071) 589 1725
Neal Street East, 4 Neal Street, London WC2   (071) 240 0135
Nihon Token, Japanese Antiques, 23 Museum Street, London WC1   (071) 580 6511
Oriental Bronzes Ltd. (Christian Deydier), 96 Mount Street, London W1   (071) 493 0309
Orion Antiques, Stand A1011, Grays Mews Market, Davies Street, London W1   (071) 629 5476
Peacock Indonesian Shop, 8 Ferdinand Street, London NW1   (071) 267 0296
The Peeking Hippo, 47 Palliser Road, London W14   (071) 381 4837
Richard and Robert Peters, 84 Portobello Road, London W11 (by appointment)   (071) 258 3554
Remote Trading, Unit 4, Mercury Works, 4 Leysfield Road, London W12   (081) 746 0049
Miranda Rothschild   (071) 727 5819
David Salmon, Holme Cott, Nr Newton Abbott, S. Devon   03643205
The Shoji Co., Lawrence Yard, Lawrence Road, London N15   (081) 809 7907
Snapdragon, Terracotta and Chinese Pots, 268 Lee High Road, London SE13   (081) 852 0296
Spink & Son Ltd, 5–7 King Street, St James's, London SW1   (071) 930 7888
Henry Woods-Wilson, 105 Onslow Square, London SW7   (071) 584 4836

Auction houses and the showrooms and galleries of specialists and dealers are fascinating places to visit, and a rich source of both goods and inspiration for the would-be Oriental stylist.

United States

West Germany

Auctioneers

Index

Page numbers in bold refer to illustrations

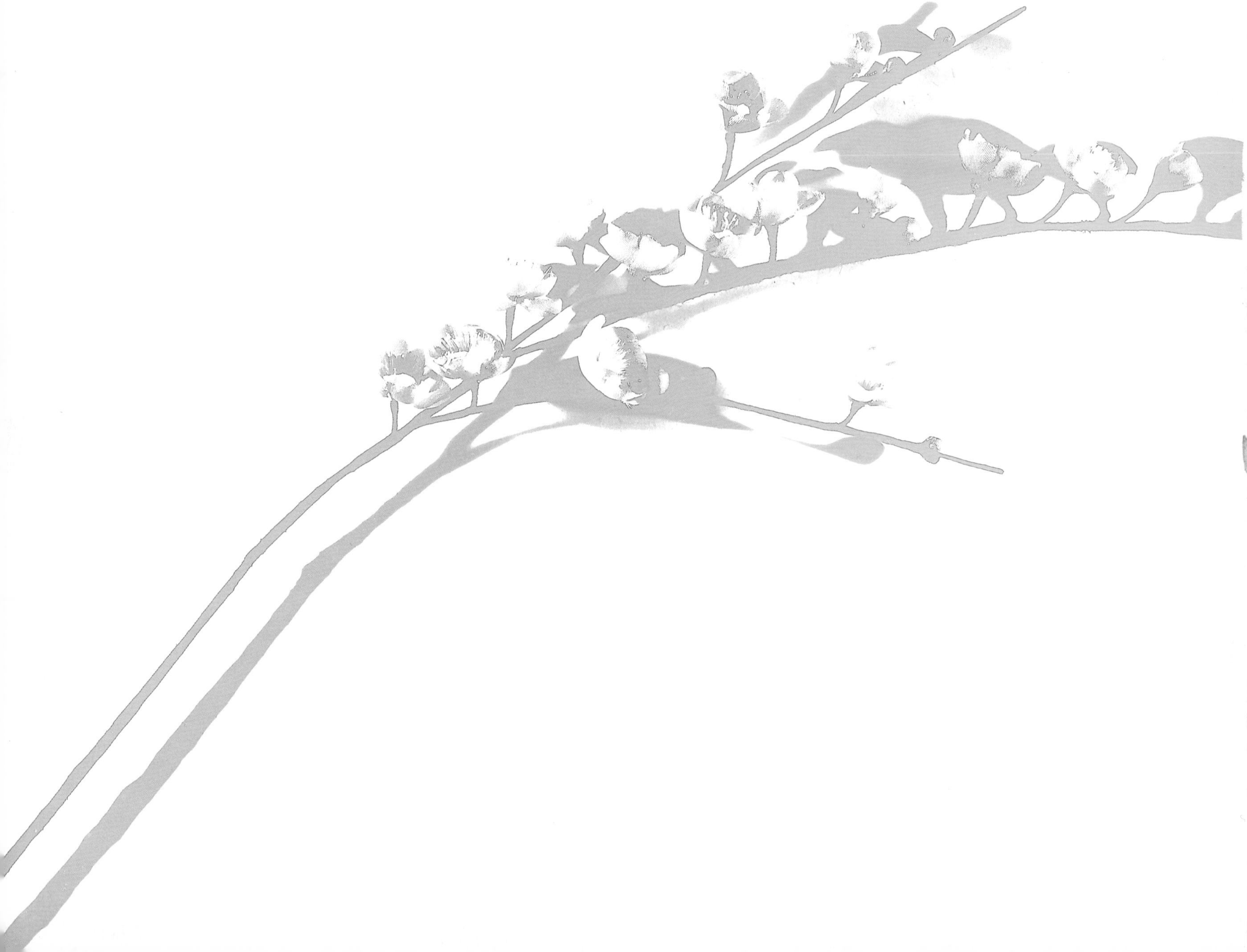

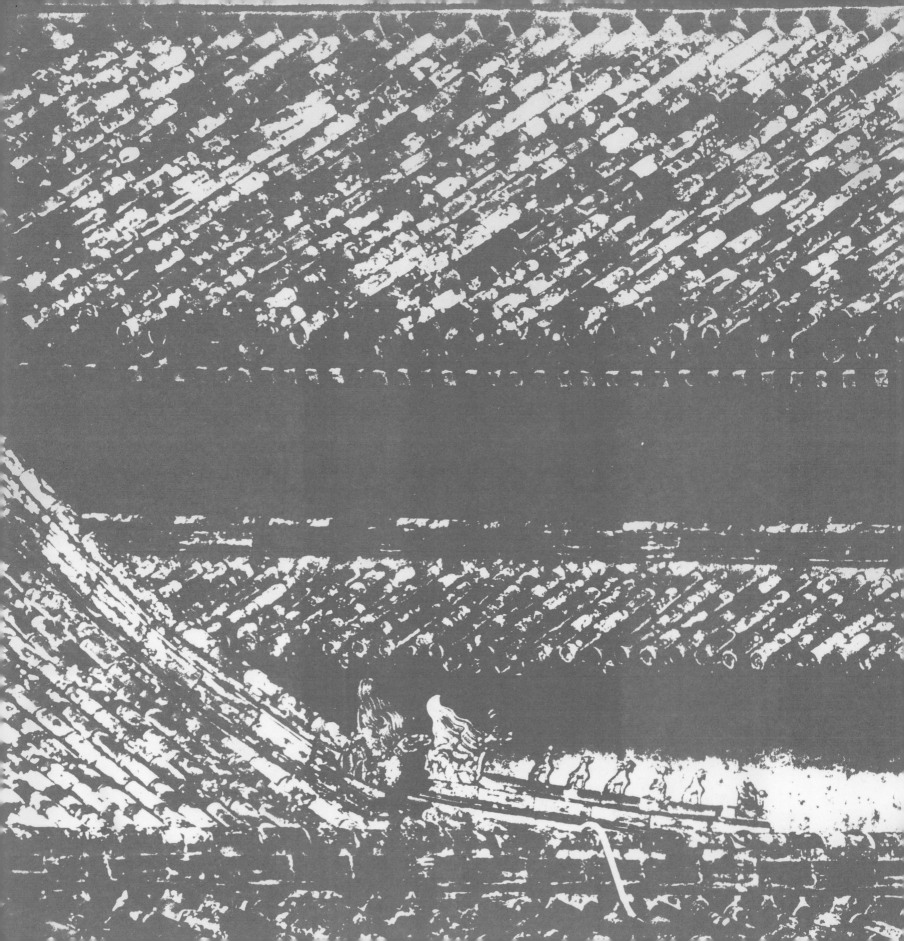